April 5, 2009

Christopher,

Enjoy years of trading.

Love, The Quines

MW01029919

Take Me Out to the Ball Game

Take Me Out to the BALL GAME

The Story of the Sensational Baseball Song

AMY WHORF McGUIGGAN

Foreword by Mike Veeck

University of Nebraska Press | Lincoln and London

4/09

For Christopher —

Amy Whorf McGuiggan

Library of Congress
Cataloging-in-Publication Data

McGuiggan, Amy Whorf, 1956–
Take me out to the ball game : the
story of the sensational baseball song /
Amy Whorf McGuiggan ; foreword by
Mike Veeck.
p. cm.
Includes bibliographical references.
ISBN 978-0-8032-1891-8 (cloth : alk. paper)
1. Von Tilzer, Albert. Take me out to the
ball game. 2. Popular music—United
States—1901–1910—History and criticism.
3. Baseball—United States—History.
4. Music and baseball. 5. Norworth, Jack.
I. Title.

ML3477.M38 2009
782.42′155—dc22   2008038059

Set in Quadraat by Kimberly Essman.
Designed by Ashley Muehlbauer.

For Jake, who lives for this . . .
and for the "team" who believed

Take Me Out to the Ball Game

Words by Jack Norworth
Music by Albert von Tilzer

Katie Casey was baseball mad,
Had the fever and had it bad;
Just to root for the hometown crew,
Ev'ry sou Katie blew.
On a Saturday, her young beau
Called to see if she'd like to go,
To see a show but Miss Kate said, "No,
I'll tell you what you can do."

Take me out to the ball game,
Take me out with the crowd.
Buy me some peanuts and Cracker Jack,
I don't care if I never get back,
Let me root, root, root for the home team,
If they don't win it's a shame.
For it's one, two, three strikes, you're out,
At the old ball game.

Katie Casey saw all the games,
Knew the players by their first names;
Told the umpire he was wrong,
All along good and strong.
When the score was just two to two,
Katie Casey knew what to do,
Just to cheer up the boys she knew,
She made the gang sing this song:

Take me out to the ball game,
Take me out with the crowd.
Buy me some peanuts and Cracker Jack,
I don't care if I never get back,
Let me root, root, root for the home team,
If they don't win it's a shame.
For it's one, two, three strikes, you're out,
At the old ball game.

Contents

Foreword by Mike Veeck   xi

Acknowledgments   xiii

Introduction: Up with the Curtain;
On with the Show   xvii

1   The Early Years: A Brief History
of Baseball   I

2   The New Century   II

3   Ladies and Gentlemen, Please
Take Your Seats   19

4   1908: The Year of the Song   39

5   Baseball and Music   51

6   Take Me Out to the Ball Game:
The Sensational Baseball Song   61

7   Let Me Hear You Good and Loud . . .
A-one, A-two, A-three   89

8   Baseball as Vaudeville   99

9   Exit Smiling   113

Bibliographic Essay   119

Foreword

MIKE VEECK

Before you a lovely blue sky melts into a dreamlike Christmas green as players in a Nureyev-like dance stretch, play catch, and watch the people in the stands as they lazily rise to their feet and begin to sing "Take Me Out to the Ball Game." The scene is reenacted in thousands of places around the world every day (or night), yet it never seems replicated. It is a brand new effort each and every time. How is that possible? Because it is a cosmic blend of just the right touches of the human spirit, all that is good about mankind—free expression, individualism, a social experience, the joy of a childlike refrain extended to the heavens, an offering to the gods in thanks for this perfect moment, this wonderful game. We are again children—carefree, laughing actors all caught in the moment. With apologies to Shakespeare, all stadiums are our stage. At the moment we shout, sing, or chant "and it's one, two, three . . . ," all is right with the world.

Speaking of the heavens, somewhere over the rainbow Harry Caray and Bill Veeck are watching this ritual and looking at each other with the grand bemusement that was the basis of their relationship. Caray, the ultimate performer (the show must go on), the reporter who never got over his rapture with the stars who played the game he so loved, wearing his heart on his sleeve and showing a youthful exuberance to create an insouciance that was both real and embellished. Veeck, a wizened, character-filled visage powered by elfin blue eyes, who had an uncanny sense of what will play with an audience. A sort of Everyman sensibility driven by an indefatigable curiosity about people. A lover of foibles and the "curiosities" that make up a man's character, his essence. A wisdom born of failures.

Amy McGuiggan has crafted a book that is scholarly and eminently readable, and that is no small feat. She makes us care about Jack Norworth and the song of which he was undoubtedly proud. Woven around the story of vaudeville, the book portrays baseball as a metaphor for life.

There are no churches here. The rapture created is the sheer joy of the human spirit—that which makes us human.

For years writers from Will and Ariel Durant to Jack Kerouac have sought to describe history in understandable terms. Amy McGuiggan has taken a subject of seemingly limited interest and placed it in a larger context, a difficult task for any writer.

Oh, about that rainbow? Veeck looks at Caray, they shrug, get to their feet, and sing at the top of their lungs "at the old ball game." After all, they are immortalized. What the hey, let's all stand and join 'em.

I'll never sing this song quite the same way again. Neither will you.

Acknowledgments

Because relatively little has been written and published about vaudeville or "Take Me Out to the Ball Game," I relied heavily on the kindness and expertise of librarians, archivists, curators, and theater historians who helped me piece together, bit by bit, the story of "the sensational baseball song." They dug deep into their offline catalogs, print collections, and newspaper morgues to find pieces for my puzzle. For their extra effort, and for access to the extraordinary visual resources of so many institutions, I am most grateful.

My deepest thanks go to staff members at the Library of Congress, The Rucker Archive/Transcendental Graphics, the Milton S. Eisenhower Library at Johns Hopkins University, the New York Public Library and its Billy Rose Theatre Division, the Berkshire Athenaeum, the National Baseball Hall of Fame and Museum and A. Bartlett Giamatti Research Center, the Omaha Public Library, the Museum of the City of New York, the Boston Public Library, The Bostonian Society, the Brooklyn Public Library/Brooklyn Collection, the Thomas Edison National Historic Site, Archeophone Records, the Chicago Historical Society, the Radio Hall of Fame/Museum of Broadcast Communications, and Manhattan College.

Numerous correspondents indulged my questions as I built the framework for this story. They include Sam Brylawski and David Seubert at the University of California–Santa Barbara, who generously searched the Victor discography for recordings of "Take Me Out to the Ball Game;" Professor Rick Altman at the University of Iowa, whose expertise in the area of vaudeville and song slides helped guide me in the early stages; Michelle Bailey, who painstakingly reviewed the Keith/Albee Archives at the University of Iowa; staff members of the local history department of the San Francisco Public Library, who sent me a copy of the 1888 poem "Casey at the Bat" as it appeared in the San Francisco Daily Examiner; Mark Linton, president of the Laguna Beach Little League; Fredric Woodbridge Wilson, curator of the Harvard Theatre Collection; Annette Marotta of the New York Public Library Billy Rose Theatre Division, who kindly researched the offline collections in preparation for my visit; June Koffi, outreach librarian for the Brooklyn Public Library, whose willingness to search *Brooklyn Daily Eagle* microfilm provided me with several crucial pieces of information; theater historian John Kenrick, whose website Musicals101.com was an invaluable part of my vaudeville education, and without whose patience and guidance I could not have burrowed into the mindset of the vaudevillian; and the late Mr. Skip Caray, who so generously corresponded with me about his dad. To all of them, I am forever grateful.

I am also grateful to all of the archivists of yesteryear who had the foresight to transfer newspapers and magazines to microfilm, and to the overcrowded and underfunded libraries that nevertheless manage to find space for hundreds of microfilm reels. I could not have written this story without the *New York Times*, maintained by the Thomas Crane Public Library in Quincy, Massachusetts; *Variety* magazine and the *New York Clipper*, maintained by the Boston Public Library; and the *Brooklyn Daily Eagle*, maintained by the New York State Library in Albany, which kindly sent me reels so that I could read the turn-of-the-century issues in the comfort of my hometown library.

Thanks to my friends Edwina and Margaret Li, concert pianists extraordinaire, who generously broke down "Take Me Out to the Ball Game" and helped me to understand it from a musical point of view.

I am grateful to my editor, Rob Taylor, at the University of Nebraska Press, who has given me the opportunity to share this colorful, never-before-told story. His professional guidance, patience, good nature, and enthusiasm for the story's nostalgia helped make the publishing process a real joy. Thanks too to everyone at University of Nebraska Press who had a hand in shaping and designing the book, including project editor Joeth Zucco, copyeditor Sandy Crump, and publicity manager Kate Salem.

Finally, two veteran baseball men who have heard "Take Me Out to the Ball Game" sung more times than they can remember have graciously lent their names to this project. The legendary broadcaster Ernie Harwell read the manuscript before anyone else and didn't hesitate to offer his kind words for the book jacket. Mike Veeck's beautiful words in the book's foreword transcend the day-to-day business of modern baseball and remind us "of all that was once good and could be again." I thank them both for going to bat for me and hope that I can repay the honor one of these days.

Introduction
Up with the Curtain;
On with the Show

Why do we sing "Take Me Out to the Ball Game" when we're already there?
AUTHOR UNKNOWN

What is it about this game of baseball—this game that plays out slowly, with no imposed time limit, until the last out is recorded—that our romance with it begins in early childhood and stays with us, like little else does, throughout our life? Is it the game's elegant design, its orderliness, the mystery and magic of its sacred numbers? Is it the game's time-honored rituals, its indelible stories, passed from one generation to another, its stories of heroes—men forever boys—bigger than the ballparks in which they played, heroes in crisp uniforms cavorting, with balletic grace, in the thick, dew-soaked pile, heroes stirring the chocolate earth inside a summer's heat or under the sliver of a summer moon? It cannot be a coincidence that the first place where baseball was played in the United States was a place called the Elysian Fields. The ancient Greeks had their own Elysian Fields, a mythical place assigned to the blessed and heroic after they died, a place of ideal happiness.

The game, the professional game at least, is now played more often than not under artificial lighting, on artificial turf surrounded by steel and concrete, plunked down in the midst of teeming urban landscapes. Yet if only in our imagination, there is still in a baseball field the vestige of a bygone America—and our own bygone youth. Baseball fields are still mythical places, places with the power to quiet the mind and soothe the heart, places of ideal happiness.

If we need evidence that baseball and its heroes have always held a special place in the lives of Americans, we need look no further than the work of artists—filmmakers, songwriters, composers, poets, writers,

This Currier and Ives print shows "the American National Game of Baseball, Grand Match for the Championship at Elysian Fields." (Currier & Ives, circa 1866. Courtesy of the Library of Congress, LC-DIG-pga-00600.)

and painters—arbiters of the public taste who have celebrated the game since its inception. No other sport has enjoyed so intimate a relationship with creative artists, who for more than a century have tried, as surrogates for the rest of us, to convey their feelings about the game and to define baseball's magical hold.

Of all the arts, music shares a special relationship with baseball. Hundreds of songs have been written about baseball since the earliest known composition was penned in 1858, but only one has held onto the hearts of fans through the generations. Other songs had their heyday, rhythmically dancing through the heads of a generation and ever present on the parlor piano, but most are now forgotten by all except students of baseball music and collectors of sheet music. "Take Me Out to the Ball Game" is the exception. Not only is it a song that has stood the test of time, it is *the* song—among the broad array of baseball polkas, waltzes, schottisches, and galops written to celebrate teams, players, and the game itself—that has come to define the national game. It is rightfully called baseball's anthem.

Entitled "Who Picks First," this photograph shows kids choosing sides for a sandlot game, 1920. (Courtesy Rucker Archive/ Transcendental Graphics.)

"The Base Ball Polka" composed by J. R. Blodgett, is the earliest known piece of base-ball music. (The Lester S. Levy Collection of Sheet Music, Special Collections, Sheridan Libraries, The Johns Hopkins University.)

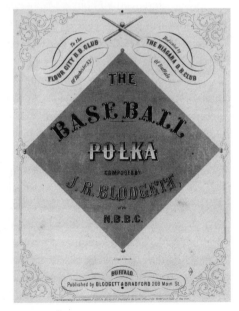

Dashed off, with accompanying doodles, on a scrap of paper during a New York subway ride by Jack Norworth, a vaudeville song and dance headliner who, it was said, had never attended a professional baseball game, "Take Me Out to the Ball Game," with music by Tin Pan Alley composer Albert von Tilzer (who also had never attended a game), was debuted on a vaudeville stage in April 1908. In no time it became a hit, inspiring robust sales of the sheet music. In the weeks following the song's debut, so many other vaudevillians had apparently "borrowed" it for their acts that Norworth was forced to abandon it in his. Or so the legend goes.

Baseball songs that followed "Take Me Out to the Ball Game," some with similar titles (such as the 1909 song, "I Want to Go to the Ball Game"), hoped to work the same magic on audiences—to be handed down, like the game itself, from one generation to the next. But most were weak imitations that struck out and never enjoyed anywhere near the same success. Even one of the era's most prolific and acclaimed song-writers, Broadway luminary George M. Cohan, who wrote "The Yankee Doodle Boy," "Give My Regards to Broadway," and "Over There"—all of which hit grand slams with audiences—couldn't find the same success with a baseball tune.

A century after Von Tilzer's publishing company, the York Music Company, published "the sensational baseball song," it is the rare person, baseball fan or not, who cannot hum or sing its catchy chorus, although few know the song's first and second verses or why, in fact, we sing "Take Me Out to the Ball Game" when we're already there. The song ranks eighth on the National Endowment for the Arts top songs of the twentieth century—sandwiched between the *West Side Story* original cast album and "You've Lost That Lovin' Feeling," a hit for the Righteous Brothers. Only "The Star Spangled Banner" and "Happy Birthday" are sung more often.

For decades, singing "Take Me Out to the Ball Game" has been a seventh-inning stretch tradition at baseball parks from coast to coast. For fans, the song has all the color of the game and creates an instant nostalgia, a yearning for a simpler time when, like Norworth's heroine, Katie Casey—the ultimate "rooter," who saw all the games and knew the players by their first names—the nation had baseball fever and had it bad. Like baseball teams and individual players, who are measured against those who came before them and will come after them, every baseball song, past and future, is measured against "Take Me Out to the Ball Game." And so far, after a century, the song's impressive streak remains unchallenged.

Take Me Out to the Ball Game

1

The Early Years:
A Brief History of Baseball

The one constant through all the years, Ray, has been baseball. America has rolled by like an army of steamrollers. It's been erased like a blackboard, rebuilt and erased again. But baseball has marked the time. This field, this game, it's a part of our past, Ray. It reminds us of all that once was good and it could be again. TERENCE MANN, *Field of Dreams*

Who invented baseball? In 1905 the Mills Commission, headed by baseball pioneer Abraham Gilbert Mills and six other distinguished gentlemen, including two U.S. senators, all of whom had impeccable baseball credentials, was convened to answer that very question.

The 1906 issue of *Spalding's Official Base Ball Guide* noted that in the previous year's guide a disagreement had arisen "as to the origin of the American National Game of Base Ball, between the veteran Base Ball writer, Mr. Henry Chadwick, and Mr. A. G. Spalding, the latter claiming that Base Ball was distinctively of American origin, while Mr. Chadwick contends that it was of English origin." The guide added that the "question as to the real origin of Base Ball has created widespread interest, especially from old timers."

Albert Goodwill Spalding held an honored place in baseball. At one time a star player, team manager, and team president, he later became a successful entrepreneur, founding a sporting goods emporium (which supplied the official baseballs for the game) and introducing a baseball guide. *Spalding's Official Base Ball Guide*, first published in 1877, became the recognized authority and arbiter for all baseball-related matters. Its editor

Abraham Gilbert Mills headed a commission that had the task, in 1905, of determining the origins of the game of baseball. (Photography Collection, Miriam and Ira D. Wallach Division of Art, Prints and Photographs, The New York Public Library, Astor, Lenox and Tilden Foundations.)

Baseball veteran and entrepreneur Albert Goodwill Spalding argued that baseball was a distinctly American game. (Photography Collection, Miriam and Ira D. Wallach Division of Art, Prints and Photographs, The New York Public Library, Astor, Lenox and Tilden Foundations.)

was that "veteran Base Ball writer" Henry Chadwick, an Englishman who argued that baseball had evolved from the English game of Rounders, a bat-and-ball game he had enjoyed as a boy.

On December 30, 1907, the Mills Commission (whose members had been handpicked by none other than Spalding) issued its final report. Published in the 1908 issue of *Spalding's Official Base Ball Guide*, the report stated: "The first scheme for playing baseball, according to the best evidence obtainable to date, was devised by Abner Doubleday at Cooperstown, N.Y. in 1839."

Henry Chadwick's family had emigrated from England in 1837 and settled in Brooklyn, where the teenage Chadwick enjoyed watching local cricket matches, then the dominant sport in the still young and ethnically English America. By the mid-1850s Chadwick, who had been a piano and guitar teacher and a composer of light music, had embarked on a career in journalism, following in his father's footsteps.

While covering cricket matches across the Hudson River in Hoboken, New Jersey—first for the *Spirit of the Times* and the *New York Times*, and later for the *New York Clipper*, a sports and theater weekly—he saw baseball being played and recognized its similarity to the Rounders of his childhood. Smitten with the game, he would devote his life to promoting it, editing the annual *Beadle's Dime Baseball Player*—the first series of baseball guides—for twenty years, authoring various how-to books and a glossary of baseball terms, and introducing the box score and the statistical game of baseball that would make it possible, in the decades to follow, for every team and player to be measured relative to another. When Chadwick died in Brooklyn in 1908, his obituary remarked that he had rendered valuable service to the national game and referred to him as the Father of Baseball. There was a certain irony in that honor; the same commission that had sprung from the Spalding/Chadwick disagreement had anointed another gentleman, Abner Doubleday, the Father of Baseball.

The English game of Rounders dates to Tudor times (King Henry VIII) and perhaps earlier, and like baseball, it is a game played by teams with a bat and ball. After hitting the ball, the batter, if he was not put out by a

Veteran baseball writer Henry Chadwick argued that baseball had evolved from English stick-and-ball games such as Rounders. (Photography Collection, Miriam and Ira D. Wallach Division of Art, Prints and Photographs, The New York Public Library, Astor, Lenox and Tilden Foundations.)

thrown ball, ran around four bases or pegs—often topped with a piece of paper so they could be readily seen—to score a rounder, the equivalent of the modern-day home run. A schoolboy version of Rounders was brought to the United States by English immigrants and, like other bat-and-ball games (One-Old-Cat and Stool-Ball, for example), spread throughout the towns of the burgeoning nation. Towns, often isolated from one another, adopted their own versions of the game and devised their own rules—thus the name Town Ball.

One youngster who played Town Ball in his hometown of Ballston Spa, New York, some fifty miles from Cooperstown, was Abner Doubleday, who was born in 1819. Doubleday, the grandson of a Revolutionary War veteran, attended school in the bucolic village of Cooperstown and went on to a distinguished Civil War military career after graduating from West Point in 1842. The story is often told that while Doubleday was stationed at Fort Sumter in Charleston, South Carolina, in 1861, he fired the first Union shot of the Civil War. His service earned him the rank of major-general and military honors for his burial at Arlington National Cemetery in 1893.

A little more than a decade after Doubleday's death, the written testimony to the Mills Commission by Colorado mining engineer Abner Graves, who had attended school with Doubleday in Cooperstown, stated that Doubleday had "invented" baseball in 1839 by making changes to the game of Town Ball—most notably, replacing the "out goal" with four bases and naming the game "Base Ball."

The "American game of 'Base Ball,'" wrote Graves, "was invented by Abner Doubleday of Cooperstown, New York, either the spring prior, or following the 'Log Cabin & Hard Cider' campaign of General Harrison for President, said Abner Doubleday being then a boy pupil of 'Green's Select School' in Cooperstown, and the same, who as General Doubleday won honor at the Battle of Gettysburg in the 'Civil War.'" Graves ended his letter to the commission by noting that "'Baseball' is undoubtedly a pure American game, and its birthplace Cooperstown, New York, and Abner Doubleday entitled to first honor of its invention."

As the Baseball Hall of Fame in Cooperstown suggests in one of its early baseball exhibits, Abner Doubleday might have earned the distinction by default. Abner Graves's letter was apparently the most appealing story to come before the Mills Commission, which, in considering the "evidence," overlooked one pesky fact: Doubleday had been a student at West Point in 1839. Indeed, baseball historians now question whether Doubleday ever actually saw a baseball game.

If its origins remain in question, there is no doubt about baseball's growing popularity in the years after 1840. By 1845 the sport was becoming America's most popular outdoor pastime. In September of that year, at Elysian Fields in Hoboken, Alexander Cartwright, a New York bank teller and volunteer fireman, organized a baseball club, the Knickerbocker Base Ball Club, and formalized a set of rules (twenty in all), including the appointment of an umpire, the creation of fair and foul territory, and the three-strike, three-out rule. The following summer the first "real" baseball game was played, with Cartwright's rules, at Elysian Fields, the same field that Henry Chadwick would report from a decade later.

By 1849 waves of Americans were leaving behind all that was familiar

NEW-JERSEY.

Base Ball.

A pretty match between the Eagle and Empire Clubs was played yesterday at Hoboken. Empire was declared the winner by two runs and certainly played the best. A good many visitors were on the ground, and the ladies took great interest in the game. The Eagles play the Gothams at the Red House, Harlem, Friday, 22d inst. Commence at 3 o'clock.

This 1855 *New York Times* article reports on a game in Hoboken, New Jersey, where Henry Chadwick first saw baseball being played.

to seek their fortune in California. Alexander Cartwright was one of those "forty-niners" who headed west to hunt gold. As he made his way across the United States, he taught the game of baseball, with his New York rules. He eventually settled in Hawaii, where he died in 1892.

The popularity of baseball coincided with what one *New York Daily Times* reporter of the day called "an undiminished ardor and enjoyment in the manly and healthful sports of the field," including cricket, as well as a general "taste for open air amusements," including boating, fishing, and "pedestrianizing." There is no reason in the world, noted the writer, why they "should not, and every reason why they should, one or the other of them, come into general and habitual use in every city and village of the United States."

By the late 1850s there were more than fifty baseball clubs in Manhattan, the city Cartwright had left a decade earlier. As Americans spread west, so too did baseball. The New York game—with the rules of the Knickerbocker Club—emerged as the preferred form of the game, but in Massachusetts the older game of Town Ball, with its square field and stakes (instead of bases) at each corner, survived longer than it did elsewhere. In 1858 rules and regulations for the Massachusetts Game were adopted, and the following year the first intercollegiate game

This 1791 Pittsfield, Massachusetts, bylaw is perhaps the earliest reference to baseball in America. (Berkshire Athenaeum, Pittsfield, Massachusetts.)

was played, using those rules, between Williams College and Amherst College in Pittsfield, Massachusetts. The city of Pittsfield would add another chapter to baseball lore in 2004, when an ancient 1791 town bylaw, one of the earliest references to baseball in America, came to light: "For the Preservation of the Windows in the New Meeting House ... no Person or Inhabitant of said Town, shall be permitted to play at any game called Wicket, Cricket, Baseball, Football, Cat, Fives, or any other Game or Games with balls, within the distance of Eighty Yards from said Meeting House."

In 1859 a Massachusetts company published *The Baseball Players' Pocket Companion*, which contained rules and regulations for playing the Massachusetts and New York games. The small book was evidence, as one writer noted in 1912, of the "existence, in a lively form of a popular appreciation of the National game in Boston and many suburban towns in the days when our grandfathers were young and participated in the sport."

In the years after the Civil War, soldiers who had played the game in camp carried its rules with them as they returned home to every corner of the country. Although baseball was still an amateur game, an upper-class gentleman's game, one *Brooklyn Daily Eagle* reporter sounded an alarm in August 1867, when he wrote:

> During the past seven years, the game of Base Ball has attained to the importance of a national amusement. It has received every encouragement from the press and public sentiment as a healthful, manly recreation, improving the physical development without detriment to the morals of our young men. . . . But grave abuses are beginning to creep in, which, if not checked, must change the whole character of the ball ground and bring it down to the level of the race course. The great element of popularity of base ball thus far has been the belief that the clubs were composed of young men who played to amuse themselves and improve their leisure hours. This was formerly true, but the champion matches, at first the result of an honest spirit of emulation, have begotten a new order of things;—base ball playing from a mere recreation is becoming a business.

English-born Harry Wright, the son of a cricketer and himself a cricketer, is credited with organizing, in 1869, the first professional team of salaried players, the Cincinnati Red Stockings. However, one original member of that team, who, on the occasion of the passing of Henry Chadwick, mysteriously signed his name as "Hasbeen" in a 1908 letter to the editor of the *New York Times*, cited 1866 as the date of the first salaried club and noted that there were many other professional teams in the east at that time. One Harry Ellard replied to Hasbeen, disputing his claim and arguing that the Cincinnati baseball nine of 1869 was indeed the very first *complete* professional baseball team in the country. Disagreement aside, the era of baseball as a business had begun in the post–Civil War period.

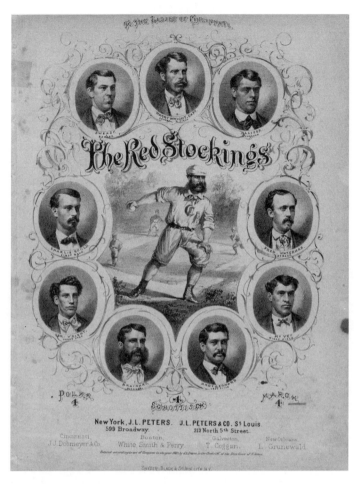

This 1869 piece of sheet music celebrated the Cincinnati Red Stockings, considered to be baseball's first all-salaried, professional team. (The Lester S. Levy Collection of Sheet Music, Special Collections, Sheridan Libraries, The Johns Hopkins University.)

The National Association of Professional Baseball Players, baseball's first professional association, was formed in 1871, and in 1876 the first league of teams, the National League, was inaugurated with eight teams. The league's president was the Honorable Morgan G. Bulkeley, who would later serve on the Mills Commission.

Not until 1901 would a rival league—the American League—be established, and two years later the two leagues squared off against one another in baseball's first World Series. By 1908 baseball had more or less assumed its modern design, and as with the nation itself, all that remained was for the diamond in the rough to be polished to a luster.

2

The New Century

Baseball is an allegorical play about America, a poetic, complex and subtle play of courage, fear, good luck, mistakes, patience about fate and sober self-esteem (batting average). It is impossible to understand America without a thorough knowledge of baseball. Artist SAUL STEINBERG

As the twentieth century dawned, echoes of the Civil War and the old America could still be heard across the land. Although much of the nation remained remote and isolated, the decade between 1890 and 1900 was, as historians have noted, a watershed decade, a decade when much of the nation was settled. Transcontinental railroad lines, completed in 1869, joined the physical edges of the country, and Americans' urge to push further westward, to exert their Manifest Destiny on the continent, had been satisfied. If America's West had been won, the thirst for adventure and the urge to explore and conquer had not been satisfied; they found new expression overseas in colonialism.

At the turn of the century Americans faced the daunting challenge of integrating a vast geographical region—rural and urban, mountain, plains, and coast—and uniting a burgeoning population whose many ethnic groups harbored deep-rooted ill will toward one another. The task of uniting the heterogeneous nation would fall to several institutions that served as agents of acculturation, institutions that helped the polyglot population become Americans. Most everyone, regardless of language or heritage, could share in and find common ground in public education, the Stars and Stripes, baseball, and the new entertainment called vaudeville.

After the assassination of William McKinley in the fall of 1901, Vice President Theodore Roosevelt, hero of the Spanish-American War, assumed the presidency. McKinley and Roosevelt had campaigned on a prosperity platform—a full dinner pail—and Roosevelt reasserted that populist pledge by promising Americans a "Square Deal." (Interestingly, in the fall of 1908 disgruntled baseball writers, demanding permanent press box facilities, invoked Roosevelt when they asserted, "A square deal from baseball is all we want." By October of that year, the Baseball Writers Association of America had been founded.)

The America that the youthful, energetic, and optimistic Roosevelt inherited was an America poised on the threshold of dramatic industrial progress and equally dramatic social change, but underlying the vigor, vitality, and confidence was another America, an America of contradictions. The nation's "democracy" excluded many, most egregiously African Americans, who were still marginalized and struggling for acceptance long after European immigrants had been assimilated. Industrialization, for all the prosperity and opportunity it brought to some, brought others only hardship and misery. The new machines that liberated so many from tedious, time-consuming tasks enslaved others.

Between 1900 and 1910, more than nine million nonwhite, non-English-speaking Italians, Slavs, Jews, and Poles, fleeing persecution and poverty in their homelands and lured by the promise of prosperity and opportunity in the United States, arrived destitute after a harrowing journey, with little more than a bundle of precious family heirlooms. Like the Irish before them, these "huddled masses" were herded through stockyard-like pens at Ellis Island in New York, where the sick, disabled, and mentally incompetent were weeded out and returned to the despair they had fled only weeks earlier.

Those who passed inspection were given new, easier to pronounce, anglicized names. Some immigrants continued their journey to the Midwest, where opportunity awaited in the mines, steel mills, and stockyards, but most settled in eastern cities (along with waves of rural Americans who were leaving the farm), working seventy-hour weeks in textile mills and garment-making sweatshops. Living in squalid, company-owned ghettoes of tenement housing (such as those on New York's Lower East Side), where sounds and smells drifting from the dingy apartments defined the neighborhoods, immigrants were paid barely a subsistence wage, twenty-two cents an hour, an average weekly wage of twelve dollars. To help them make ends meet, their employers extended credit through the company store, but this served only to keep laborers forever in debt and dependent. As a means of controlling workers and discouraging strikes, management pitted one ethnic group against another. It was, as historians have noted, industrial serfdom.

In the rural South, the situation was hardly better. For African Americans who had been emancipated after the Civil War, the 1875 Civil Right Acts came with the promise of equality and opportunity—until it was overturned in 1883. In 1896 African Americans experienced yet another setback when the landmark Supreme Court case *Plessy v. Ferguson* upheld distinctions based on race. The Court approved legally enforced segregation, provided that the facilities and accommodations for African Americans were not inferior to those for whites. Jim Crow laws (named for an 1830 white minstrel performer named Thomas "Daddy" Rice, who, while wearing blackface, presented a program of plantation songs and dances that shaped the stereotypical image of black laziness and inferiority) codified the subordination of African Americans. In the post–Civil War era, slavery had simply been replaced by institutionalized racism.

The system of white supremacy and special privilege that limited economic advancement and personal freedom for African Americans had its parallel not only in the North, where white urban factory owners subordinated nonwhite European immigrants, but also around the globe, in the form of colonial imperialism. On the backs of labor, on the backs of the oppressed, industrial tycoons—robber barons—built powerful railroad, banking, financial, and steel monopolies as well as vast personal fortunes. As the eminent historian Alistair Cooke noted, a handful of men controlled the resources of each continent.

But if many in the United States had not yet realized the fundamental rights and citizenship guaranteed by the Founding Fathers or the promise of the new industrialization, there was nevertheless a sense of optimism in turn-of-the-century, Progressive Era America—a belief that they too might one day share in the American Dream. And change was indeed in the air.

The sheer number of new Americans challenged the white, Protestant status quo. Women were emerging, and although most still fulfilled the role of traditional homemaker, many were entering the work force in white-collar office and government jobs. With their new buying power, women demanded political power. Laborers too demanded that their voice be heard. They protested the inhumane conditions in which they and their children were forced to live and work. Anarchists, who argued that the system was unfair to the working man, championed their cause.

In 1909 a black northerner named W. E. B. DuBois, no longer willing to accommodate the oppression endured by African Americans, founded the National Association for the Advancement of Colored People. Although Jim Crow laws and minstrelsy perpetuated stereotypes and fed bigotry, African Americans dreamed of a promised land. Their spirituals sang always of freedom and dignity.

Despite its social ills, turn-of-the-century America was the most prosperous nation on earth. With the financial turmoil of the mid-1890s behind them, Americans saw the future in a bright light. An extraordinary range of fin de siècle accomplishments had been on view at the World's Fairs that were visited by millions of Americans in cities such as Chicago, Omaha, Buffalo, and St. Louis between 1893 and 1904. Progress was the mantra of the day. Scientific and technological breakthroughs had given Americans all sorts of marvelous new inventions—the camera, the phonograph, the automobile, the radio, the telephone, the movie projector, and the airplane—although for the time being they were luxuries that only the very wealthy could afford.

Skyscrapers, bridges, and electric lighting were transforming cities, as were rapid transit systems. Boston built the first subway in 1897, New York followed in 1904, and Philadelphia in 1905. Not only could folks go out into the lighted night, now they were no longer confined to their own neighborhoods or to where they might travel on foot.

Along the subway lines, away from the festering slums of the inner city, new ethnic neighborhoods and new business opportunities emerged, just as new towns and cities—and new opportunities—had emerged along the transcontinental railroad thirty years earlier.

One of the attractions at Omaha's 1898 Trans-Mississippi & International Exposition and other early World's Fairs was the electric light display. Electric lights were transforming turn-of-the-century cities and providing opportunities for after-dark entertainments. (From the collections of the Omaha Public Library [TMI 00298].)

With concessions from employers—a shortened work week, safer working conditions, and a decent living wage—and with affordable factory goods and labor-saving machines flooding the marketplace, turn-of-the-century Americans had something they had never had before: leisure time and a little extra money in their pockets. Even for the working class, life was no longer a constant toil. And to fill their leisure time, upwardly mobile Americans were taking vacations and asking to be entertained.

Those who chose to stay at home enjoyed games, crafts, and sing-alongs around the parlor piano, a symbol of good taste and refinement in the early twentieth century. Nearly every aspect of life was celebrated in song, and the insatiable appetite for new songs spawned an American sheet music industry known as Tin Pan Alley. Songs were written one day and available in sheet music a few days later at the five-and-dime store. Millions of copies were sold every week.

Despite squalid conditions, kids living in New York's tenements still found a way to enjoy the national game. (Photo by Lewis Wickes Hine. Photography Collection, Miriam and Ira D. Wallach Division of Art, Prints and Photographs, The New York Public Library, Astor, Lenox and Tilden Foundations.)

The more adventuresome American, inspired by the example of President Roosevelt and his doctrine of the "strenuous life," was taking to the great outdoors—getting back to nature. As cities grew filthy and congested, urban planners recognized the need for fresh air, recreation, and relaxation, and they set aside parklands and public gardens for leisurely strolls, picnics, roller skating, band concerts, and ball games— pastoral pastimes reminiscent of the rural life that had become a quaint relic, captured in Currier and Ives prints, and for which many twentieth-century Americans began to yearn.

For those who could afford to get away, respite was sought in the mountains, by the stream, and at the shore. Newspapers of the day offered page after page of advertisements for summer playgrounds— "physician recommended!"—where one could find pure air, pure water, pure milk, shaded avenues, no malaria, and "health at a moderate cost."

And wherever Americans traveled, popular amusements were waiting to satisfy their seemingly insatiable appetite for fun.

Traveling circuses, rodeos, water parks, arcades, and storefront nickelodeons (where for five cents patrons could see moving pictures, "flicks," and illustrated song slides) all vied for Americans' leisure time and precious disposable income. Entertainment was becoming big business, and no entertainment would become bigger business than vaudeville and baseball.

But vaudeville and baseball were more than just entertainment, more than just business. The vaudeville theater and the baseball field were social laboratories where the great melting pot experiment was conducted; where Irish, Jews, African Americans, Italians, and Slavs mixed and mingled, observed one another, learned from one another, and tried on new ideas; and where a sense of community was fostered within what seemed to be a fractured America.

3

Ladies and Gentlemen, Please Take Your Seats

Oh, don't worry about the critics. You got a smash hit. It's in the air, kid, it's in the air. You can't stop anything that's in the air. GEORGE M. COHAN, *Yankee Doodle Dandy*

If baseball evolved rather than being invented, so too did the new entertainment—vaudeville—that took the United States by storm in the last decade of the nineteenth century and throve until the era of radio and moving pictures. For half a century vaudeville was the entertainment choice for the populace.

Although many theater historians date vaudeville's demise precisely to the autumn of 1932, when New York's big-time Palace Theatre discontinued vaudeville and began featuring motion pictures (it didn't help that it was also the start of the economic deprivation of the Great Depression), movies had already been captivating audiences for decades, ever since Thomas Edison first experimented with them in the early 1890s and lent his name to the marketing of a new machine, the vitascope, which could project moving images in large theaters. (By 1896 Edison had invented his own projector, the kinetoscope.) Turn-of-the-century audiences were naturally attracted to this latest novelty, and moving pictures soon became the much-anticipated, indeed expected, filler between acts in vaudeville houses. Theater managers, apparently unaware of the potential impact of the new medium, never imagined that the vitascope and kinetoscope, which they so proudly advertised on the bill with other live acts, would be responsible, at least in part,

P. T. Barnum's American Museum in New York, shown here circa 1850, was an early dime museum where patrons could take in plays and bizarre exhibits for ten cents. Such "museums" would influence vaudeville entertainment years later. (Picture Collection, The Branch Libraries, The New York Public Library, Astor, Lenox and Tilden Foundations.)

Impresario Tony Pastor cleaned up men-only entertainment and enticed women and children into the theater with his "tasteful" and "polite" acts and with door prizes such as home goods. Pastor made his professional singing debut at P. T. Barnum's American Museum in 1846. (Billy Rose Theatre Division, The New York Public Library for the Performing Arts, Astor, Lenox and Tilden Foundations.)

Tony Pastor's Fourteenth Street Theatre, shown here in 1895, was located next door to Tammany Hall. Financial problems and a changing entertainment landscape in New York forced Pastor to close his "famous amusement resort" in 1908. (Museum of the City of New York, Byron Collection, 41.420.503.)

for the death of vaudeville. In time it was the vaudeville act that became the novelty filler between movie reel changes.

Borrowing a little from English music hall entertainment, Wild West shows, minstrel shows, medicine shows, traveling circuses, dime museums, beer hall entertainment, the Yiddish theater, and burlesque, vaudeville was the name for an affordable, "respectable" variety entertainment that catered to a broader slice of American society than traditional entertainment for men only.

In 1881 New York theater manager Tony Pastor, who had cut his entertainment teeth as a circus clown, introduced a form of variety that was free of risqué material, lewdness, and profanity—for the more refined tastes of upwardly mobile working Americans—especially women, whom he enticed into his always-packed Fourteenth Street Theatre with door prizes such as food staples and home goods. The introduction of "tasteful" entertainment in New York—a teaming, pulsating cauldron of diversity and the mecca of big-time entertainment—coincided with a broader community reform movement determined to clean up "lowbrow" Bowery entertainment as well as political corruption and uncivilized beer-hall behavior at baseball games.

Other theater managers, recognizing the same opportunities as Pastor, also cleaned up their acts to attract a new and diverse audience (from whom management also demanded polite behavior). None would be more powerful or influential than circus-performer-turned-entrepreneur Benjamin Franklin Keith, a New Hampshire native who, along with Edward Franklin Albee, a Maine native and also a graduate of the circus game, created a vaudeville empire of hundreds of theaters spread across America.

It is Keith who is often credited with coining the word *vaudeville*, which is said to derive from *Vau de Vire*, a French region in Normandy known for its light, popular, satirical songs. Others trace the word to *voix de ville*, meaning voice of the city. It was often said that the vaudeville stage did indeed have as many voices as the city.

In 1883 Keith opened his first theater, The Gaiety, in Boston—a dime museum filled with animal and fossil specimens and curiosities that patrons could view for ten cents. On the museum's second floor a small

This early handbill advertising vaudeville includes an enticement for women and children. (Courtesy of the Library of Congress, LC-DIG-nclc-04787.)

Benjamin Franklin Keith, with partner Edward F. Albee, created a vaudeville empire of hundreds of theaters that stretched across the United States. (Courtesy of the Boston Public Library, Print Department.)

Edward Franklin Albee, together with business partner B. F. Keith, formed the United Booking Office (UBO), which controlled the bookings for most of the vaudeville circuits. (Courtesy of the Boston Public Library, Print Department.)

"WHERE ARE YOU GOING MY PRETTY MAID?" KEITH'S "I'M GOING TO SIR", SHE SAID.

VAUDEVILLE

This theater poster, circa 1905, advertises Benjamin Keith's Vaudeville. Keith and Edward Albee built a vaudeville empire. (Created by W. J. Morgan & Co. Lith., Cleveland, OH. Courtesy of the Library of Congress, LC-USZC4-4959.)

theater offered variety entertainment. By 1885 Keith had taken over management of the Bijou Theatre, where his concept of continuous vaudeville, a twelve-hour bill of entertainment (changing weekly) in which acts appeared two, three, or even four times throughout the afternoon and evening, allowed patrons to stop in as their work or shopping schedules permitted. A decade later, in 1894, in the heart of Boston's business and shopping district, Keith opened B. F. Keith's New Theatre, a big-time dream palace of comfort, elegance, and gentility.

Across America, theater managers built independent vaudeville houses as well as chains (circuits) of big-time, small-time theaters (like the Orpheum chain, named for Orpheus, the Greek god of music and poetry), small time, and even small-small-time theaters—more than five thousand by 1910. Like the industrial resources of the continent, the major circuits were managed by a handful of tycoons (sometimes referred to as vaudeville industrialists) who, led by Keith and Albee, organized to form a central booking office that controlled the salaries and routes, indeed the livelihoods, of performers. If for performers it was a form of artistic indenture, it was also an insurance policy, providing them with regular work for up to forty weeks each year, and often for two or more years.

Vaudeville theaters in small towns were little more than storefronts whose managers paid performers fifteen to twenty-five dollars a week, but in big-time theaters in the heart of America's great cities (like Hammerstein's Victoria in Manhattan), performers might be paid as much as five hundred dollars a week.

Like Keith's New Theatre, the new generation of big-time theaters, which adopted a two-a-day performance schedule, were escapes from reality—magical, self-contained worlds that spoke to the aspirations of middle-class America by offering opulent architecture, marble sculpture, plush rugs, ventilation, lavish scenery, a house orchestra, and a "crackerjack" bill of nine premier acts for a dollar seat on the floor. Balcony seats were cheaper, as was the entertainment in small-time houses, where patrons could take in a continuous show (quantity over quality) for as little as ten cents.

And it was a kaleidoscopic show, with entertainment ranging from

Adams House and Keith's
Theatre, Washington St.,
Boston, Mass.

Keith's Theatre, shown here circa 1907–15, was located in the heart of
Boston's shopping district. Its matinee performances catered to shoppers.
(The Bostonian Society, Old State House, Postcard Collection ca. 1898–1945,
vw0053/005721.)

The Couture Brothers and other contortionists were always a popular act on any vaudeville bill. (Billy Rose Theatre Division, The New York Public Library for the Performing Arts, Astor, Lenox and Tilden Foundations.)

animal acts; ventriloquists; mimes; male and female impersonators; bicycle and swimming acts; jugglers; and contortionists to harmonica, violin, banjo, ukulele, accordion, spoon, and piano players; escape artists; exotic dancers; celebrity cameos, duets, trios, and family acts; comedy monologues; dramatic skits; ethnic humor; and spoofs on current events. Like the new department stores that were sprouting up everywhere in cities, the vaudeville stage had something for every audience member— for the young and the old, for working folks, for middle-class women and children, and for newly arrived immigrants.

For African American and immigrant performers—particularly the Irish, who had grown accustomed to being told they need not apply, and the Jews, who had been Europe's scapegoat—the vaudeville stage offered opportunity they might not otherwise have had, a way out of the dire poverty that they and earlier generations had known. Ethnic differences seemed to matter less if one could entertain and amuse, although differences unfortunately still mattered. In the segregated United States, African American performers were separated from others backstage; and African American and white patrons were segregated in the theater. As theater historian John Kenrick notes, "There were instances of blacks buying orchestra seats, only to be told by management that their seats were actually in the balcony."

Jewish performers, indeed performers of all ethnic backgrounds, routinely changed and anglicized their names (one impoverished Lower East Side lad, Moses Schoenfeld, became Lew Fields), not necessarily because they feared prejudice, although they certainly knew it existed, but to fit in, to be more American. According to Kenrick, "If even a small element of a given audience was less likely to be receptive because a performer had a Jewish sounding name, then why fight them?" The same held for Italians, Germans, Hungarians, and anyone else who thought they might have a fairer chance with a new and simpler name. "The key factor in the vaudevillian mindset," says Kenrick, "was the need to make a living." Performers did whatever it took.

The great paradox of vaudeville (and a source of great consternation for modern sensibilities) was that ethnic performers too often fed the very same prejudice that they hoped to avoid with their new identities. African American and immigrant vaudevillians routinely got laughs with the broadly drawn stereotypes of laziness, confusion, and ignorance that white America used to justify its continuing exploitation, oppression, and segregation. However, the self-lampooning also served as a way for ethnic groups, who were naturally suspicious of one another, to be introduced to one another's "curious ways." Ethnic stereotypes were not as offensive and unacceptable to turn-of-the-century audiences as they would be today. "Ethnic pride," notes Kenrick, "was much less of a factor one hundred years ago. With so many groups living cheek by jowl in crowded cities, ethnic slurs and insults were part of daily conversation. If you wanted to survive, you had to be able to both dish it out and take such slurs, and vaudeville reflected that." Vaudeville was, says Kenrick, an "equal opportunity insulter." Virtually no one was immune to on-stage satire, although particularly pernicious insults (by turn-of-the-century standards) were condoned neither by audiences nor by theater management.

Racial and ethnic material, theater historians have suggested, was far more complex and sophisticated than it appeared. Performers masterfully presented acts that could both poke fun at their own circumstances and subtly manipulate ethnic stereotypes to expose their exaggeration and false premise. And all the while the performers were artfully showcasing their unique talents. Only decades later, and after hard-won political, moral, and legal victories, were African American and immigrant performers finally able to celebrate their authentic cultures and folkways, not parodies of them.

If vaudeville was an equal opportunity insulter, it was also an equal opportunity employer. Even "performers" with no real talent could find success on the stage if they could amuse and please. No matter that one had little or no legitimate singing, dancing, or comedic skills; if a performer could work up an act, especially a novelty act such as plate spinning, backward writing, crying, or sneezing, there was a place on the vaudeville bill. Mail-order courses for aspiring vaudevillians promised to turn anyone into a bicycle trick rider or a barrel-jumping, punching-bag, or mind-reading expert.

A typical vaudeville bill adhered to a specific, tried-and-true formula of brief (except for the headliner, no more than fifteen minutes or the audience might get bored), self-contained acts (so that they could be easily removed or inserted into a bill), beginning with a silent act (a juggler, for instance) to usher in arriving patrons, followed by a singing act (perhaps a duet) to settle the crowd. A good comedy sketch was next, to "wake up" the audience, followed by an even better act, perhaps a fully staged skit, which anticipated the "name" act who closed the first half, the second best spot on the bill.

The part two opener (the sixth spot on the bill) as well as the seventh spot on the bill might be either a comedy skit with ethnic humor or a dramatic skit. Then came the act everyone had waited for, the headliner, the next to last act and the premier spot on the bill. The show concluded with an exciting finish such as an acrobat or trapeze artist. In houses that featured continuous entertainment rather than the two-a-day schedule, the last act, the chaser, was often one so dull that it chased the audience from the theater so that a new audience could be seated.

It was a nomadic and often lonely life for the twenty thousand performers who made vaudeville their career, a life in which the better part of every year was spent on the road on various big-time or small-time circuits. (Everyone aspired to making the big time or to being discovered for a "legitimate" and classy Broadway show or revue, although fewer than ten percent ever made it.) They lived in boarding houses and did the same act over and over and over again, night after night after night in city after city after city, polishing and perfecting it based on the responses of audiences who demanded that performances be fresh and sincere. Variously described as unpretentious, egotistical, naïve, self-confident, guileless, envious, adaptable, temperamental, and savvy, these vaudevillians were, more than anything, hardworking.

For audiences, an afternoon or evening at the vaudeville was a personal, interactive experience. In the days before microphones and amplification, performers spoke directly to patrons in the house. Successful performers knew how to establish a sense of intimacy and rapport with their audience, a sense of their being let in on something private and special. No one who hoped to continue in the business or to make the big time could ever get away with simply "mailing it in," to use a modern expression. Every day, twice a day, they played it like they had never played it before.

If theater managers (who could make or break a career with their performance reports to circuit moguls like Edward Albee) counted on performers to fill seats and boost box office receipts, the music publishers on Tin Pan Alley relied on headliners, as well as novelty acts looking for a little background music, to sell their songs. Vaudeville and Tin Pan Alley went hand in hand, and performers, particularly headliners, who were always eager for new material to spruce up their act, routinely stopped in at the music publishing companies (some called them mills) on Tin Pan Alley. Salesmen escorted performers to soundproof rooms where they plugged the trendiest songs (with topical themes that were often "ripped from the headlines") and assisted the performers in polishing songs for their acts. The vaudevillian left with a "professional" copy of the song, complete with orchestration, and if the publisher was lucky and the song went over well that night, audiences would leave the theater humming the tune on their way to the five-and-dime to buy the sheet music.

Albert von Tilzer was the younger brother of famed hit-maker, Harry von Tilzer. In 1903, Albert opened his own music publishing company, the York Music Company. Five years later he published "Take Me Out to the Ball Game," for which he composed the music. (Billy Rose Theatre Division, The New York Public Library for the Performing Arts, Astor, Lenox and Tilden Foundations.)

Jack Norworth's "The College Boy" was the act in monologue that made Norworth a star. (Billy Rose Theatre Division, The New York Public Library for the Performing Arts, Astor, Lenox and Tilden Foundations.)

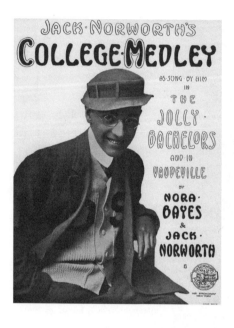

This 1910 sheet music cover features Jack Norworth's "College Medley," the charming medley of hits that had made Norworth a vaudeville favorite years earlier. (The Lester S. Levy Collection of Sheet Music, Special Collections, Sheridan Libraries, The Johns Hopkins University.)

Among the many pioneering tinsmiths of the alley was Harry Gumm (1872-1946). Born in Indiana to Jacob Gumm, a German immigrant shoe-store owner, Harry left home at fourteen to join the Cole Brothers Circus. A self-taught pianist, Gumm changed his name to Von Tilzer—his mother Sarah's maiden name with "Von" added for an aristocratic touch—and in 1892 moved to New York, where he began writing songs and playing piano in saloons. In 1898 he had his first hit, "My Old New Hampshire Home," written with lyricist Andrew B. Sterling, and by 1902 he had opened his own publishing company, where he continued to publish his own songs, including "Wait 'Till the Sun Shines, Nellie" and "I Want a Girl (Just Like the Girl That Married Dear Old Dad)," as well as songs by others, which earned him fame as "the man who launched a thousand hits." It is said that his tinny piano inspired the name Tin Pan Alley, although other stories credit the name to the general cacophony of sound that emanated from the early publishing houses—lured by the razzle-dazzle of the Great White Way—that clustered on West Twenty-eighth Street between Broadway and Sixth Avenue.

Harry's younger brother Albert, who was born in Indianapolis in 1878, was, like his brother, a self-taught pianist, and he also changed his name to Von Tilzer (as did three other brothers, all of whom worked in the music business). Albert worked briefly in the Chicago office of his brother's publishing company and then moved to New York City, where he worked as a shoe salesman in Brooklyn while studying harmony, his first formal music training. By 1903 he had opened his own Tin Pan Alley publishing company, the York Music Company, and was composing songs for Broadway and vaudeville. In 1906 Albert von Tilzer began a partnership with a vaudeville headliner and musical comedy star named Jack Norworth, known on the circuit as Handsome Jack and the College Boy.

Norworth, born John Knauff in Philadelphia in 1879, was the son of a music teacher and organist who, hoping to discourage any show business ambitions, sent the young Norworth to sea aboard the Pennsylvania Nautical School Ship *Saratoga*. Norworth returned from sea undeterred and by 1898 he had made his debut, performing in blackface, in a New Jersey vaudeville house.

By 1903 Norworth had abandoned the burnt cork and had reinvented himself as a monologist (akin to a stand-up comic today) with a novelty act that included witty stories, songs, and jokes. A new character, the College Boy, and a medley of songs, "College Medley," helped to launch Norworth into the big time as both a performer and a songwriter. Within two years Norworth, still in his twenties, was performing at "refined vaudeville" houses and enjoying the privileges that came with being a headliner, including star billing and reviews in the weeklies.

By late 1906 Norworth, while married to his first wife—the celebrated actress Louise Dresser, with whom he had performed as early as 1901 in Brooklyn—had become infatuated with an actress and mimic named Trixie Friganza, whom Dresser complained was often at the Philadelphia theater where she and Norworth were starring in a Lew Fields show, *About Town*. Dresser asserted that Friganza (whom one writer called a "rollicking butterball") had "alienated her husband's affections."

Norworth and Friganza worked together throughout 1907 and into 1908, and they planned to marry after his divorce from Dresser became

Actress Louise Dresser was the first of Jack Norworth's five wives. (Billy Rose Theatre Division, The New York Public Library for the Performing Arts, Astor, Lenox and Tilden Foundations.)

Actress Trixie Friganza, born Delia O'Callahan, was the woman accused by Louise Dresser of stealing Jack Norworth's affections from her. (Courtesy of the Library of Congress, LC-USZ62-126271.)

A 1908 New Year's week vaudeville poster from Buffalo shows both Trixie Friganza and Jack Norworth on the bill. (Courtesy of the Library of Congress, POS-MAG-.H37, no. 5 [C size].)

final. (Friganza had tipped off a reporter in Kansas City as early as October 1907 that wedding bells would ring for the couple.) But on June 21, 1908, only a week after his divorce from Dresser, Norworth abruptly married one of the most popular, entrancing, and highest-paid, though ill-tempered, stars of the early twentieth century, the singing comedienne with the "magnetic personality" and contralto voice, Leonora "Dora" Goldberg, known by vaudeville audiences as Nora Bayes.

The newlyweds, who were said to have an "infectious stage presence," starred later that summer in the Follies of 1908—a glitzy, girlie, glamorous Broadway revue that producer Florenz Ziegfeld Jr. modeled on the Folies Bergère—for which they wrote the smash hit "Shine On, Harvest

One of the most popular stars of the vaudeville stage, Nora Bayes, married Jack Norworth in June 1908, just days after his divorce from Louise Dresser. The temperamental Bayes was often billed as "The Greatest Single Woman Singing Comedienne in the World." (Courtesy of the Library of Congress, LC-DIG-ggbain-35668.)

In September 1908, Jack Norworth joined Nora Bayes in Florenz Ziegfeld's Follies of 1908 after it moved from the Jardin de Paris to the New York Theatre. There the couple introduced their hit "Shine On, Harvest Moon." (Billy Rose Theatre Division, The New York Public Library for the Performing Arts, Astor, Lenox and Tilden Foundations.)

This *New York Times* ad touts the Ziegfeld Follies of 1908. Ziegfeld staged his elaborate theatrical productions from 1907 to 1931.

Moon." The celebrated couple traveled in limousines and private railroad cars, rented out entire floors of hotels, and earned an incredible $2,500 a week, more than two hundred times the average working wage.

But "Shine On, Harvest Moon" was not Norworth's only hit that year. With Von Tilzer, his collaborator for "Holding Hands (You Don't Say Nothing at All)" in 1906 and "Honey Boy," a tribute to the minstrel George "Honey Boy" Evans in 1907, he wrote the hit song "Smarty" in February of 1908. Described as "positively the biggest hit in the country," it wouldn't be for long.

By April Norworth had written the lyrics to another song for which Von Tilzer wrote the music. "Take Me Out to the Ball Game" would become an even bigger hit than "Smarty," and Norworth and Von Tilzer were the unlikeliest of duos to collaborate on "the sensational baseball song." Neither had ever been to a professional baseball game.

4

1908: The Year of the Song

Man, I did love this game. I'd have played for food money. It was a game. The
sounds. The smells. Did you ever hold a ball or glove to your face? I used to love
traveling from town to town. The hotels, brass spittoons in the lobbies, brass
beds in the rooms. It was the crowd, rising to their feet . . . always hit deep. Shoot,
I'd have played for nothing.   "SHOELESS JOE" JACKSON, *Field of Dreams*

The editors of Time-Life's *Our American Century* series call the decade
between 1900 and 1910 the "golden interlude," a "comfortable moment
before the good young days vanished completely and modern times
arrived at full tide."

In June 1908 the nation mourned the death of a former president,
Grover Cleveland, and in November Americans chose a new president,
Roosevelt's Secretary of War, William Howard Taft. Taft was elected
the nation's twenty-seventh president, defeating Democrat and three-
time candidate William Jennings Bryan, the anti-imperialist who had
campaigned against big money interests and monopolies and whose
sympathies had lain with the farmer and laborer.

In the art world, a group of painters dubbed "The Eight" by critics
eschewed the prevailing Hudson River painters' romantic view of the
United States and painted gritty, unsentimental scenes of everyday life
in the urbanized, industrial America. The social commentary of this
Ashcan school paralleled the work of writer Upton Sinclair, whose
novel *The Jungle* had exposed the harsh truth about the meatpacking
industry, and photographer Lewis Wickes Hine, who had focused his
camera on the shame of child labor, including children who performed

"The Four Novelty Grahams." It was not uncommon for children such as Willie and Herbert Graham, pictured here with their father, to perform with their families in vaudeville. Their mother, not pictured, was also part of the act. Turn-of-the-century photographers such as Lewis Wickes Hine documented the harsh truth about child labor, including their participation in vaudeville acts. (Photo by Lewis W. Hine. Courtesy of the Library of Congress, LC-DIG-nclc-04677 and LC-USZ62-49599.)

in vaudeville. Muckraking journalists with social consciences exposed political corruption, the sham of patent medicines, and the misery of festering urban slums.

Other newsmakers of the day included the Wright Brothers, who in 1908 set another aviation record when they sustained flight for over an hour. In October 1908 Henry Ford's simple, reliable, and mass-produced Model T rolled off the assembly line for a price—$950—that the working American could afford. By 1920 the automobile would be an established part of the nation's social and commercial travel, and by 1930 fifteen million Model Ts had been sold. Other titans of industry included James Pierpont Morgan, John D. Rockefeller, and Andrew Carnegie, a Scottish immigrant who had recognized the potential for a successful steel industry in the new America.

Illustrator Charles Dana Gibson gave Americans the Gibson girl, the idealized woman of the era. Beautiful (with her long upswept hair), self-confident, charming, and sporty, she was, if not yet liberated, at least a little more independent—with a hint of mischief—than the woman of a decade earlier.

The Bureau of Investigation, the forerunner to the Federal Bureau of Investigation, was founded in 1908. So too were the first scout troops that formed the core of the Boy Scouts of America, which became incorporated in 1910. Mother's Day, first conceived by Julia Ward Howe as a women's day for peace during the Civil War, was observed for the first time in May 1908. Pneumonia and tuberculosis were the scourges of society.

In the world of entertainment, New Yorkers mourned the death in September of Tony Pastor, the Father of Vaudeville, who three decades earlier had introduced "clean" variety to the American stage. Ehrich Weiss, the "International Jailbreaker," a Hungarian immigrant better known by his stage name, Harry Houdini, offered a thousand dollars to anyone with a device—a straightjacket, jail cell, trunk, handcuffs—from which he couldn't escape. In 1908 this Master of the Impossible performed another of his stunning escapes when, in Boston for an engagement at Keith's New Theatre, he jumped, handcuffed, from the Harvard Bridge and escaped under water in the Charles River.

The great Houdini, the "Genius of Escape," who never ceased to startle and amaze, was filmed during a daring underwater stunt in Boston in 1908. He was appearing at Keith's Theatre. (Courtesy of the Library of Congress, LC-USZ62-26518.)

Celebrated sportswriter and Vanderbilt alumnus Grantland Rice, who coached the Vanderbilt baseball team in 1908, penned the poem "Alumnus Football" in honor of the school's alumni reunion in June. Two lines of the poem, about a college football star named Bill Jones, who encounters obstacles on his journey through life, achieved instant immortality:

> For when the one Great Scorer comes to write against your name,
> He marks—not that you won or lost—but how you played the Game.

On the baseball field it was the game's Deadball Era, named for the so-called dead ball that purportedly gave an advantage to pitchers and the defense. This was also the end of the era of the wooden ballpark. Andrew Carnegie's vision for the steel industry was partially realized in 1909, when the first two concrete and steel parks were built in Pittsburgh and Philadelphia, ushering in a new, more sophisticated era of baseball.

During the Deadball Era, as Society for American Baseball Research historian David Jones has noted, stability had come to the game, "distinct from the chaotic, unruly brand of baseball played in the late nineteenth century—with its rising and falling leagues, vagabond franchises, and

This photo, entitled "The Ball Team, 1908," shows a group of glassworkers in Indiana. In the early years of professional baseball, many young men who played returned home after the season to work at jobs in factories, mines, and mills. (Lewis Hine photo. Courtesy of the Library of Congress, LC-DIG-nclc-01159 and LC-USZ6-1215.)

archaic rules." Still, writes Jones, the game "lacked a certain veneer of respectability that it would later acquire." It was a game "played by young men who grew up working in coal mines and factories, and the restrictive measures of the reserve clause ensured that, for most of them, their financial prospects never strayed far from their working class roots."

That sentiment echoed a 1908 *New York Times* article that noted that there had been

> too much rowdyism at the Polo Grounds lately, and the temper of some of the players has been unduly ruffled. A strong force of police has been needed to preserve order. This state of things is not pleasant to contemplate. Baseball has been purified of gambling [The Black Sox scandal a decade later would prove the case to be otherwise—Ed.], and it is a pity that it cannot be kept free from the suspicion of

This *New York Times* headline announcing the death, in 1908, of Henry Chadwick calls him the "Father of Baseball." The Mills Commission gave that distinction to Abner Doubleday.

intemperance, which is frequently the cause of outbreaks of violence in a crowd. It is a clean and wholesome sport, of itself, and a well-played match is an inspiring spectacle, one that attracts many refined persons of both sexes.

During the 1908 preseason, the Mills Commission published its finding that baseball was strictly an American game and had indeed been invented by Abner Doubleday in Cooperstown in 1839. As the new baseball season began, the national game lost its most ardent supporter, Henry Chadwick, who died of pneumonia at age eighty-three. His obituary called him the Father of Baseball—no empty honor, said its writer. "He was an acknowledged authority on all its technicalities. He invented the approved system of scoring. He had written enough about the game, wisely and clearly, to fill many volumes. To the very end of his life he attended baseball matches and vigorously expressed his opinion of the play; and his opinion counted."

On the field, the elegant, educated, and well-liked Christy "Matty" Mathewson and the temperamental, rough-hewn, and widely disliked Ty Cobb, the "Georgia Peach," grabbed headlines. Cobb also grabbed another kind of headline that year when he married. The Cubs' legendary combination—Tinker-Evers-Chance—grabbed headlines by turning 6-4-3 and 4-6-3 double plays and were later immortalized by Franklin Pierce Adams, who expressed the feeling of many New York fans:

The *New York Times* ran daily ads for games at the Polo Grounds. Fans could take the new Broadway line train uptown to the field.

These are the saddest of possible words,
"Tinker to Evers to Chance,"
Trio of Bear Cubs and fleeter than birds,
"Tinker to Evers to Chance."
Ruthlessly pricking our gonfalon bubble,
Making a Giant hit into a double,
Words that are weighty with nothing but trouble,
"Tinker to Evers to Chance."

Other legendary baseball figures were Cy Young, Honus "Hans" Wagner, "Shoeless Joe" Jackson (who, like Cobb, was married that year), Mordecai "Three Finger" Brown, and Walter Johnson.

At New York's fabled Polo Grounds, manager John McGraw and his Giants were enjoying a sensational year, and when it was all over in October, more than nine hundred thousand New York fans had cheered their team from the stands.

The season's highlights included a ten-inning no-hitter pitched by George "Hooks" Wiltse on July 4. On July 16 the *New York Times* "paused in the discussion of graver matters" to comment on the baseball season thus far. "It is pleasant, however, to have one of the New York nines in the running, to have their name synonymous for a time with good baseball, and to be able to feel they have a chance to get the pennant, even if in the opinion of the multitude of experts that trophy is likely to be Chicago's again. The experts may be mistaken, as experts often are. The season is young and the Giants are near the top."

GIANTS OUTSHOOT QUAKER PATRIOTS

Consequently They Are Doubly Victorious Over the Philadelphians.

WILTSE IN NO-HIT RANKS

New York Pitcher Prevents Visitors Making a Safe Smash In Morning Contest at Polo Grounds.

This 1908 *New York Times* headline reflects the Giants' successful season and a mid-season no-hitter. The 1908 baseball season would prove to be one of the most exciting of all time.

GIANTS CLIMBING NEARER THE TOP

Defeat Reds and Are Now Only Three Points Behind Cubs In Pennant Race.

MATHEWSON IS KEYED UP

Sets Cincinnati Down with Four Hits and Strikes Out Six Batsmen— Brooklyn Blanks Chicago.

A 1908 *New York Times* headline touts Giants star Christy Mathewson, the idol of every young fan.

A few weeks later, with the Giants, Cubs, and Pirates all vying for the pennant, twenty-five thousand fans—then a record crowd—packed the Polo Grounds, only to see the Giants routed by the Pirates and Honus Wagner, who went five for five. The beat reporter for the *New York Times* noted that "any one who made the mistake of getting to the grounds later than 2 o'clock met up with a lot of difficulties before getting to his claim. . . . The principal difficulty was in finding the aisles, and this was a legitimate difficulty, because there weren't any aisles."

By early August the attendance record had been shattered, as a "vast crowd" of thirty thousand fans cheered the Giants to victory over the Cubs on August 8. The Giant juggernaut rolled on into September. The city was baseball mad. The *Times* noted on September 21:

> With the multitude in this hour baseball is the uppermost topic. The recent games at the Polo Grounds have attracted crowds of from 25,000 to 30,000 vociferous spectators. The daily bulletins of news posted in public places concern many events of larger importance than the game of baseball, but the crowds around them have obviously gathered to read only the ball scores. The interest in the professional contests has been cumulative this year, because of the nearly even play of three of the National League teams, the Chicago, Pittsburgh and New York players. The chances are now all in favor of triumph for the New Yorkers, who are so far ahead that only a series of unexpected mishaps could lead to their defeat. The victory of the admirable Pittsburgh team at the Polo Grounds Saturday afternoon served to show that the pennant is not yet won.

The reporter's caution was prescient. Two days later, on September 23, the Giants, in first place by a hair, hosted the Cubs. Tied 1-1 with two out in the bottom of the ninth and Giants runners on first and third, Fred Merkle, the runner on first base, made a fatal running mistake—the "Merkle Boner"—on Al Bridwell's single. Although the runner from third scored—and victory appeared to be in the Giants' hands—Merkle failed to touch second base and instead headed for the clubhouse, believing the game had been won. As Cubs players scrambled to find a ball to complete the force-out, pandemonium broke out. Umpires ruled that

BLUNDER COSTS GIANTS VICTORY

Merkle Rushes Off Base Line Before Winning Run Is Scored, and Is Declared Out.

CONFUSION ON BALL FIELD

Chance Asserts That McCormick's Run Does Not Count— Crowd Breaks Up Game.

UMPIRE DECLARES IT A TIE

Singular Occurrence on Polo Grounds Reported to President Pulliam, Who Will Decide Case.

This *New York Times* headline reveals the now-famous "Merkle Boner," which cost the Giants a crucial game in late September.

Fans pack the Polo Grounds to see the disputed game replayed on October 8, 1908. (Courtesy of the Library of Congress, LC-DIG-ggbain-02322.)

The *New York Times* headline declared the "final battle" of the season.

the run didn't count and declared the game a tie. Because the two teams finished the season tied for first place, the disputed game was replayed on October 8. "Three-Finger" Brown beat Christy Mathewson that day to give the Cubs the pennant, a World Series berth against the Tigers, and ultimately the World Series title.

That magical 1908 season seemed to have turned every New Yorker into a Giants—and baseball—fan. The old wooden grandstand was routinely filled with celebrities, politicians, and the stars of Broadway and vaudeville. But the thrills of that 1908 season, its ecstasies and agonies, were all still months away on the April day when Jack Norworth, riding the New York subway, saw a gaudy, lithographed poster of a silk-hosed baseball player standing with a bat on his shoulder.

Although he had never been to a professional baseball game, Norworth began to write lyrics for a baseball song, and by the time he reached his destination thirty minutes later, he had penned a song about a baseball-mad girl named Katie Casey. Conceived as a romantic ballad, the song tells the story of how, when Katie's beau asks her to go to a show (vaudeville, no doubt), she, in her Gibson girl manner, asks instead to be taken out to the ball game.

Years after writing the song, Norworth was asked how he knew about baseball if he had never seen a professional game. He said he had lis-

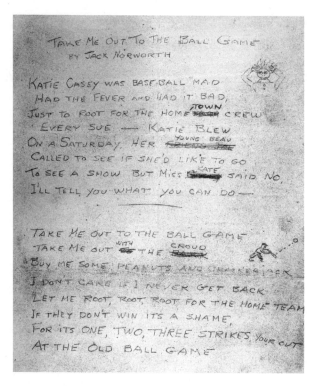

Songwriter Jack Norworth's original lyrics to "Take Me Out to the Ball Game,"
were scribbled during a subway ride. Years later, when asked why he wrote the
song, he said, "It was simply time for a baseball song." (National Baseball Hall
of Fame Library, Cooperstown, New York.)

tened and gotten the feel of baseball by watching bush (i.e., sandlot)
games as a kid. Asked why he had decided to write a baseball song, he
said that it was "simply time for a baseball song." Norworth was, after
all, a songwriter whose work, like that of all Tin Pan Alley tunesmiths,
was market driven. And in 1908 few things were driving the market
like baseball.

"The reign of bat and ball," noted one *New York Times* sports reporter,
"is supreme."

5

Baseball and Music

Music soothes us, stirs us; it puts noble feelings in us; it melts us to tears . . . it is a language by itself, just as perfect, in its way, as speech, as words; just as divine, just as blessed. CHARLES KINGSLEY

Virtually every aspect of daily life in America—love and sentimentality, war and tragedy, invention and technology, immigration, childhood, and recreation—has been celebrated in song. Songs are a reflection of the times, and if songs about Americans' pastimes are any indication of their values, ours is a nation that is, and always has been, crazy about baseball. The game's unique design and rhythm must somehow lend themselves to music, because no other sport has been the source of so much celebration in song.

Baseball music generally falls into three categories—songs that celebrate teams, songs that celebrate individual players, and songs that celebrate the game itself. Since the first known piece of published baseball music, "The Base Ball Polka," was written by J. R. Blodgett of the Niagara Base Ball Club for the Flour City Base Ball Club of Rochester, New York, and published by Blodgett and Bradford in Buffalo in 1858, hundreds of songs have tried to capture the nostalgia of the game and its hold on the American memory.

As industrialization gave Americans more leisure time and purchasing power, music publishers rushed to satisfy Americans' insatiable appetite for new songs for voice and piano. By the early nineteenth century the upright piano, which was more affordable than the earlier grander versions, was becoming a mainstay of parlors and the centerpiece of family leisure time and home entertainment. With the piano came sheet music, issued in loose sheets from four to sixteen pages long and produced quickly to capture rapidly changing events, styles, and attitudes.

The nationwide proliferation of vaudeville houses, nickelodeons, circuses, and amusement parks, where singers plugged songs for Tin Pan Alley music publishers, spawned a boom in music publishing. Audiences exited shows, humming their favorite tune on their way to the five-and-dime to buy the sheet music. The availability of affordable sheet music for pennies a song coincided with advances in printing, especially the new chromolithography process that allowed sheet music, which earlier had been printed with the intaglio engraving process, to be printed economically with eye-catching color (although many of the earlier engraved covers were equally beautiful in their detail). Great care was taken with sheet music covers: their decorative borders, stylish typography, and strong visual design, including patriotic emblems that conveyed baseball as the national game and pictures of favorite performers or baseball players, all helped to sell the song as much as the song sold itself.

For baseball fans, music has always been a part of the game, beginning from the post–Civil War era, when brass bands performed in ballparks, to the current day, when the strains of rap and rock and roll reverberate throughout stadiums during batting practice, and teams and individual players define themselves by their personal anthems.

Many of the earliest published baseball songs were instrumental pieces dedicated to local teams and written for the new dance crazes: "Live Oak Polka," published in 1860 and dedicated to the Live Oak Base Ball Club of Rochester, New York; "Home Run Quick Step," dedicated to members of the Mercantile Base Ball Club of Philadelphia, and "Home Run Galop," dedicated to the Atlantic Club of Chicago, which both were published in 1861; the "Home Run Polka," dedicated to the National Base Ball Club and published in 1867; "Una Schottische," published in 1874 and dedicated to the Una Base Ball Club of Charlestown, Massachusetts; and the "Silver Ball March," written in 1870 for the Lowell (Boston) Base Ball Club.

Several songs—a polka, a march, and a schottische—celebrated base-

This cover for "Hurrah for Our National Game," written and composed by Walter Neville, is typical of baseball sheet music covers, which often used American symbols to represent the sport as the "national game." (The Lester S. Levy Collection of Sheet Music, Special Collections, Sheridan Libraries, The Johns Hopkins University.)

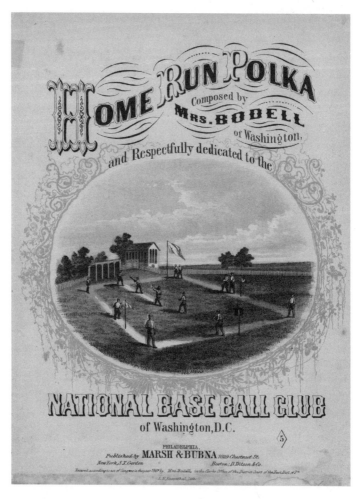

Many baseball songs, including the "Home Run Polka," were "respectfully dedicated" to ball clubs or individuals. (The Lester S. Levy Collection of Sheet Music, Special Collections, Sheridan Libraries, The Johns Hopkins University.)

ball's first professional team, the 1869 Red Stockings of Cincinnati. Others celebrated the game itself: "Catch It on the Fly," published in 1867 and dedicated to the Excelsior Club of Chicago and the Forest City Club of Rockford, Illinois; "Tally One For Me," published in 1877; and "Steal! Slide! Anyway!" written in 1889 and dedicated to the New York Base Ball Club. Still other songs celebrated legendary figures from the game: "Spalding's Base Ball Tourists Around the World," published in 1889 to celebrate Al Spalding's evangelistic, post-1888 season "All-America Team" world tour; "Slide, Kelly, Slide," published the same year and dedicated to Mike "King" Kelly, the famous base stealer; the 1904 "Husky Hans," a "stirring march and two-step," respectfully dedicated to Honus Wagner; and "Cubs on Parade," a march two-step published in 1907 and dedicated to Frank Chance of Tinker-to-Evers-to-Chance fame.

In 1908, the year that Jack Norworth and Albert von Tilzer collaborated on "Take Me Out to the Ball Game," at least eight other baseball songs, all now largely forgotten, were written. They include a song, "Take Your Girl to the Ball Game," that was advertised in its day as "a home-run hit," with words and music by one of Broadway's most prolific song and dance men, George M. Cohan, known as "the man who owned Broadway." As one sheet music sales representative from the Cohan and Harris Music Publishing Company noted during a sales call in Philadelphia, "'George M. Cohan' on a sheet of music will sell it anywhere, and he has turned out more 'sellers' of magnitude than any writer for productions I know of."

Despite an avalanche of advertising for his baseball song, and what amounted to an advertising war between Norworth's song and Cohan's, Cohan's song did not earn him the immortality that Norworth and Von Tilzer's earned them. However, Cohan would find immortality with classics such as "The Yankee Doodle Boy," "You're a Grand Old Flag" and "Give My Regards to Broadway."

In 1910 Albert von Tilzer tried his hand at another baseball song, "Back to the Bleachers for Mine," but like so many baseball songs, it failed to captivate the public in the way that "Take Me Out to the Ball Game" had. His brother, Harry von Tilzer, who wrote the 1905 hit "Wait 'Till the Sun

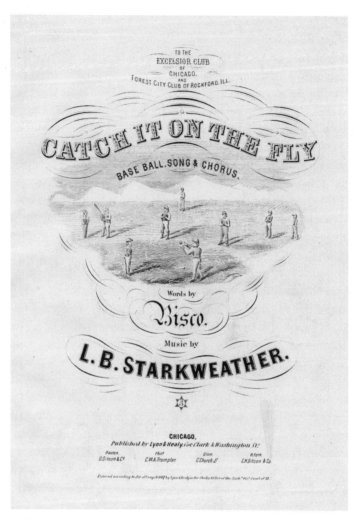

"Catch It on the Fly" and other baseball songs celebrated the game itself as well as a number of its star players. (The Lester S. Levy Collection of Sheet Music, Special Collections, Sheridan Libraries, The Johns Hopkins University.)

Sheet music covers for baseball songs, such as this one for "Tally One for Me," often incorporated the design of the baseball diamond to sell the charm of the game. (The Lester S. Levy Collection of Sheet Music, Special Collections, Sheridan Libraries, The Johns Hopkins University.)

The famous base stealer Mike "King" Kelly had his own baseball song, as did Honus Wagner, Frank Chance, and later stars of the game such as Joe DiMaggio and Mickey Mantle. (Courtesy Rucker Archive/Transcendental Graphics.)

Shines, Nellie," tried writing baseball songs, including the 1911 "The Base Ball Glide," with Andrew B. Sterling, but without success.

Norworth himself tried again in 1909 with a song, "Let's Get the Umpire's Goat," cowritten with his wife, Nora Bayes. According to the Harvard Theatre Collection archivist, the song was possibly conceived as a sequel or follow-up to "Take Me Out to the Ball Game." "Let's Get the Umpire's Goat" was introduced during the Ziegfeld Follies of 1909, in a baseball skit set at the Polo Grounds that featured Jack Norworth as an umpire. The Follies of 1909 also introduced another baseball number, "Come On, Play Ball with Me Dearie," written by Ed Madden and

Gus Edwards, who have been credited by some theater historians with ghostwriting "Shine On, Harvest Moon" for Norworth and Bayes.

If few remember Katie Casey, the heroine of "Take Me Out to the Ball Game," fewer still remember the protagonist of "Let's Get the Umpire's Goat," young Jimmy Croker (a nod, perhaps, to the infamous Tammany Hall political boss Richard Croker), a "clerk for a broker . . . who kept wishin . . . in fact his ambition . . . was to be like Giants outfielder, Mike Donlin."

6

Take Me Out to the Ball Game:
The Sensational Baseball Song

No baseball fan has to explain his mania to any other baseball fan. They are a fraternity. It is less easy, often it is hopeless, to try to explain it to anyone else. You grow technical, and you do not make sense. You grow sentimental, and you are deemed soft in the head. How, the benighted outsider asks you with no little condescension, can you grow sentimental about a cold-blooded professional sport? JOHN K. HUTCHENS

A testament to the emergence of women as the new century approached can be found not only in the nascent suffrage movement and the sheer number of bold, big-time, big-money diva singers, actresses, and comediennes who populated vaudeville but anecdotally in, of all things, baseball music. The 1889 hit "Slide, Kelly, Slide!" composed by J. W. Kelly, was written for the celebrated vaudeville songstress and comedienne Miss Maggie Cline. The 1895 baseball song "Who Would Doubt That I'm a Man?" was dedicated to "the new woman."

In May 1908 the prolific George M. Cohan, who had already scored hits with "The Yankee Doodle Boy," "Give My Regards to Broadway," "You're a Grand Old Flag," and "Harrigan," published "Take Your Girl to the Ball Game." The sheet music cover depicted a well-dressed, turn-of-the-century Gibson girl watching a game with her beau. That same month, Jack Norworth's "Take Me Out to the Ball Game," a song meant to be sung by a woman, featured a spunky young lady named Katie Casey, who asks, in the song's first verse, which is rarely sung and little known, to be taken out to the ball game instead of to a show, which is

J. W. KELLY'S SONG.

SLIDE KELY SLIDE.

SUNG BY **MAGGIE CLINE.**

❀❀ | 4 | ❀❀

NEW YORK.
Published by Frank Harding.

Musical Million, 39 Wych Street, Strand, London, England.

A misprint on the sheet music cover didn't take away from the appeal of Mike "King" Kelly's song, sung memorably by Maggie Cline, a renowned vaudeville singer and comedienne whose specialty was Irish songs. (The Lester S. Levy Collection of Sheet Music, Special Collections, Sheridan Libraries, The Johns Hopkins University.)

No one before or since George M. Cohan, also known as "the man who owned Broadway," has rivaled his personality, talent, and prodigious output. By 1908 he was at the top of his game. (Billy Rose Theatre Division, The New York Public Library for the Performing Arts, Astor, Lenox and Tilden Foundations.)

why we sing "Take Me Out to the Ball Game" when we're already at the game!

It has long been debated just who Katie Casey was, and it has been suggested that she was Norworth's girlfriend at the time the song was written. With his divorce from Louise Dresser pending, Norworth's attentions were focused on actress Trixie Friganza in the spring of 1908. However, in June, with little publicity, Norworth abruptly married vaudeville star Nora Bayes, who had made her name in 1902 with a merry Harry von Tilzer song, "Down Where the Wurzburger Flows." It was the second marriage for both Norworth and Bayes, and together the Bayes/Norworth team, billed as "America's Happiest Couple," became one of vaudeville's most celebrated and imitated songwriting and performing couples until their divorce in 1913.

So if Katie Casey was not Norworth's girlfriend, could she have been an homage to, or perhaps a blatant attempt to capitalize on, the famous

1888 poem "Casey at the Bat," popularized by vaudeville star DeWolf Hopper, who performed the poem more than ten thousand times? It appears that one of the first recordings of "Casey at the Bat" was made in 1906, just two years before Norworth penned his song. Norworth undoubtedly would have been familiar with the poem. Was he also familiar with the song, "I Don't Care If You Never Come Back," popularized by the legendary team of Bert Williams and George Walker?

As was often the case in the competitive world of vaudeville, where performers were always trying to outdo and upstage one another and where backstage drama was the norm, if an act was successful, it was routinely "borrowed" by other performers. The impulse to ride the coattails of another's success (or simply to antagonize the other) may explain not only Norworth's attempt to capitalize on the "Casey" cachet but also why, in 1927, twenty years after giving the baseball world his Katie Casey, Norworth revised his song's original lyrics, changing his heroine's name to Nellie Kelly. Was it mere coincidence that a few years earlier, in 1922, George M. Cohan had scored a hit with his musical *Little Nellie Kelly*, which enjoyed a Broadway run of 248 performances?

But capitalizing on the commercial success of *Little Nellie Kelly* was probably not Norworth's only reason for the revision. Norworth and Cohan had history dating back twenty years. In 1917 Nora Bayes, by then divorced from Norworth, had made Cohan's patriotic song "Over There" a smash hit. But the true David and Goliath encounter had come in 1908, when Norworth's baseball song, "Take Me Out to the Ball Game," published by Von Tilzer's company, the York Music Company, and Cohan's "Take Your Girl to the Ball Game," published by the Cohan and Harris Publishing Company, had gone head to head in an advertising war for the public's affections.

Both numbers were written as stand-alone novelty songs, not as part of a musical production or revue, as many songs of the day were. At the start of the baseball season in mid-April, neither songwriter could have known how riveting the 1908 baseball season would be, especially for New Yorkers, or how perfect a backdrop that season—which all came down to one final playoff game between the Giants and the Cubs—would be for their songs.

As is the case with baseball's beginnings, some details about "Take Me Out to the Ball Game" are difficult, probably impossible, to pin down. There was an old adage in vaudeville that went something like this: Keep moving, change your name and your past, and embellish your stories. It was a kind of laissez faire attitude and mythmaking that explains, in part, both the difficulty in tracking the whereabouts of any particular performer and the discrepancies in the various accounts of a performer's personal history and professional career.

Few in vaudeville, as in early baseball, gave much if any thought to the future or their legacy. Record keeping was sporadic (individual songs were rarely listed for vaudeville bills, although they were listed for musical productions and revues, such as the Follies), and relatively little documentation survived the decline of vaudeville in the 1930s. There were no archives to preserve materials relating to the performing arts. Indeed, as musical theater historian John Kenrick notes, there are still theater scholars who do not consider "tawdry" musical theater such as vaudeville worthy of preservation, making the piecing together of its history all the more challenging and frustrating. What was saved was saved by accident or because it happened to appear in newspapers.

However, it is known that the two verses and the chorus of "Take Me Out to the Ball Game" were written in the key of D major as a waltz, in a pulse of three with the strong beat on the first beat and the weaker beats on two and three. From a musical point of view, it is a simple song, with catchy, forward-moving phrases and repetition, a song typical of those that made vaudeville a phenomenon. A simple melody will always linger, noted the prolific songwriter Irving Berlin, who, as a teenager, worked for Harry von Tilzer.

"Take Me Out to the Ball Game" was said to be an instant hit when it was introduced, although there seems to be some discrepancy as to where, when, and by whom the song was debuted. Various accounts have the song being introduced during the 1908 baseball season; others place the debut in the postseason. One of those postseason accounts claims that the popular singer Billy Murray, "the Denver Nightingale," released the song with the Haydn Quartet in September 1908. Although Murray did in fact perform with the Haydn Quartet, music historians have determined that he was *not* singing with the quartet when it recorded "Take Me Out to the Ball Game" for Victor.

Various sources claim that the song was written for and introduced by Norworth's wife, Nora Bayes, during the Ziegfeld Follies of 1908, or by Norworth and Bayes during the same Follies. According to the Harvard Theatre Collection archives, however, there is no mention of the song in the 1908 Follies program.

In October 1908 a *Philadelphia Inquirer* article discussed the marriage of Norworth and Bayes and noted that Mr. Norworth had been commissioned earlier in the year to write special songs for Miss Bayes and the Follies. (Both had appeared, along with George M. Cohan and Albert von Tilzer, at a benefit on February 23, 1908. At the time, Norworth was "infatuated" with Trixie Friganza.) The article listed several of the songs Norworth had written for his own vaudeville act, including the hit "Smarty," which was published in February (perhaps Norworth and Von Tilzer performed it at the benefit), as well as songs he had written for Bayes, including her Follies hits "You Will Have to Sing an Irish Song" and "Since Mother Was a Girl." "Take Me Out to the Ball Game" was not mentioned in the story.

Numerous accounts have Norworth introducing the song on his own at Brooklyn's Amphion Theatre, where it reportedly "struck out" during an afternoon performance but went over rather well at the evening performance. The audience "ate it up," Norworth is reputed to have said of the evening performance. Still another account has Albert von Tilzer introducing the song in vaudeville.

In the late 1950s Norworth, then in his late seventies, gave an interview in which he remembered introducing the song at Hammerstein's Victoria (the top vaudeville house for years until the Palace Theatre opened in 1913), where he headlined regularly and where, on the song's first night, he recalled, it went over "pretty good, and then it got so big they began fighting over it." "They" were the other vaudevillians, who thought nothing of "borrowing" from one another. As a headliner, Norworth appeared next to last on a nine-act bill. Not long after he introduced "Take Me Out to the Ball Game," so many performers before him were

Hammerstein's Victoria Theatre of Varieties, built in 1899, first introduced its audiences to vaudeville in 1904. Jack Norworth was a regular at the theater, considered the top vaudeville venue in New York until the Palace Theater opened in 1913. (Museum of the City of New York, Theater Collection.)

apparently singing the song in their acts that Norworth eventually abandoned the song in his.

So when, in fact, did "Take Me Out to the Ball Game" make its debut? And which song came first, Norworth's "Take Me Out to the Ball Game" or Cohan's "Take Your Girl to the Ball Game?" The pages of *Variety*, vaudeville's trade magazine, the *New York Clipper*, the popular sports and entertainment newspaper for which Henry Chadwick had written decades earlier, the *Brooklyn Daily Eagle*, and the U.S. Copyright Office document some of the story.

In the May 2, 1908, issues of *Variety* and the *New York Clipper*, bold display ads first appeared for Norworth's "Take Me Out to the Ball Game" (confidently billed as "Jack Norworth and Albert von Tilzer's latest summer waltz song craze") and Cohan's "Take Your Girl to the Ball Game" (the "novelty summer waltz song and a home run hit"). A second ad for

JACK NORWORTH and ALBERT VON TILZER'S LATEST SUMMER WALTZ SONG CRAZE

"TAKE ME OUT TO THE BALL GAME"

The York Music Co., **ALBERT VON TILZER, Mgr.,** 40 West 28th Street, NEW YORK

UP TO THE SECOND!——THE NOVELTY SUMMER WALTZ SONG

"Take Your Girl TO THE Ball Game"
A HOME RUN HIT
By GEO. M. COHAN——WM. JEROME——JEAN SCHWARTZ
THIS SONG IS NOW READY.   YOU'RE ALL INVITED.   COME UP AND HEAR IT.

THE COHAN and HARRIS PUBLISHING CO., 115 West 42D Bet. B'way and 6th Ave. **New York**

(Top) On May 2, 1908, *Variety* ran an ad for the "latest summer waltz song craze," "Take Me Out to the Ball Game," which was published by the York Music Company.

(Bottom) The Cohan and Harris Publishing Company responded to the ad for "Take Me Out to the Ball Game" by running its own *Variety* ad for its "novelty summer waltz song," "Take Your Girl to the Ball Game."

"Take Your Girl to the Ball Game" appeared in the same issue of *Variety*, noting that the "big song hit" was published by Cohan and Harris, the Yankee Doodle Music Publishers—no doubt an attempt to capitalize on the Cohan smash hit of 1904.

The following week, in the May 9 issue of *Variety*, an article on page eight noted the similarity between the two song titles and that the new songs had been the talk of the popular music trade the past week, although it did not mention when the songs debuted. The article concludes, "Neither of the publishing firms makes the usual claims when a similarity in theme or title arises. It is admitted that this instance is simply peculiar." But was it?

A second ad in the May 2, 1908, issue of *Variety* aimed to capitalize on Cohan's patriotic hit of 1904, "The Yankee Doodle Boy."

The May 9, 1908, issue of *Variety* called attention to the similarity of the two newly published baseball songs.

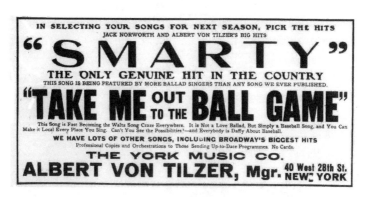

In early August 1908 the York Music Company again took out an ad in *Variety* for "Take Me Out to the Ball Game," as well as for another Von Tilzer and Norworth hit, "Smarty."

In the same May 9 issue, a display ad for the Cohan song notes that it was premiered by Miss Ethel Levey (Cohan's first wife, to whom he was married from 1899 to 1907) at Hammerstein's on May 4; and in the May 16 *Variety* the song is touted as the "summer song sensation." An ad in the May 16 issue of the *New York Clipper* calls the Cohan song "a home run hit in the first inning."

Throughout the summer and until September 5 (with the exception of a week here or there) display ads appeared in *Variety* and the *New York Clipper* for the George M. Cohan song. By June 27, illustrated song slides—"the most realistic, attractive and beautiful slides ever seen"— made at the American League ballpark by New York lantern slide maker DeWitt C. Wheeler were available for the Cohan song.

Not until the August 8 issue did another display ad for Norworth's "Take Me Out to the Ball Game" appear in *Variety*, although ads for the song did appear in May and June issues of the *New York Clipper*. The large ads, taken out by the York Music Company, promoted "Take Me Out to the Ball Game" as well as the other Norworth/Von Tilzer late winter/ early spring hit, "Smarty."

"Take Me Out to the Ball Game" was advertised as "fast becoming the waltz song craze everywhere," and by May 23, more than a month before song slides were available for the Cohan song, DeWitt C. Wheeler advertised illustrated song slides ("the most novel slides ever made") for "Take Me Out to the Ball Game." By late August another display ad from the Cohan and Harris Publishing Company noted that new verses had just been written for their song: "extra verses (straight or comic) for every city and every ball team in the league." Clearly Von Tilzer's York Music Company and the Cohan and Harris Publishing Company were engaged in their own little advertising war, and the superstar Cohan, then at the top of his game, appears to have outspent Von Tilzer. But did Cohan's investment translate into sales, and which of the songsmiths was hoping to capitalize on the other's novel idea?

On May 2, 1908, Albert von Tilzer and the York Music Company submitted "Take Me Out to the Ball Game" to the U.S. Copyright Office. A week later, on May 8, the Cohan and Harris Publishing Company submitted its song. It appears that the Goliath, Cohan, who had several hit productions on Broadway in 1908, including *The Yankee Prince* and *George Washington, Jr.* (as well as numerous hits in previous seasons), rushed out his baseball song to capitalize on the success of "Take Me Out to the Ball Game."

The question as to when Norworth's song was introduced remains unsettled, although circumstantial evidence helps to make a very sound case for a Brooklyn debut at the Grand Opera House (a long-time vaudeville house dating back to Florenz Ziegfeld's pre-Follies days when he offered ten thousand dollars to anyone who could duplicate the performance of his Strongman Sandow, "the Monarch of Muscle"!) in late April 1908—coincidentally, just days after the death of Henry Chadwick, the Father of Baseball.

Given the song's May 2 copyright and the flurry of newspaper ads, it cannot logically be claimed, as some accounts have, that the song debuted after the baseball season. In the highly competitive dog-eat-dog worlds of vaudeville and Tin Pan Alley, "Take Me Out to the Ball Game" would have debuted shortly, if not immediately, after being written, as the Cohan song had been. Indeed, a strong argument can be made that Cohan's baseball song was a response to the enthusiastic reception that Norworth's song received.

Throughout the month of March 1908, Norworth performed in

A full month before slides for George Cohan's song were ready, this ad in the *New York Clipper* announced the illustrated song slides for "Take Me Out to the Ball Game."

As this *New York Times* ad shows, Jack Norworth headlined at Hammerstein's Victoria Theatre the week of April 6 before the start of the 1908 baseball season. Although Norworth recalled in a late 1950s interview that he had introduced "Take Me Out to the Ball Game" at Hammerstein's, it is unlikely that the song had been written in time for this April engagement. Note that the bill also features the Vitagraph, the moving picture company that was formed to compete with Thomas Edison's vitascope.

DONLIN BANGS BALL OVER THE BLEACHERS

25,000 Rooters Cheer Home Run Drive That Brings Victory to the Giants.

LID OFF AT POLO GROUNDS

Bursting Sides Off, Crowd Overflows Field and Makes Life Miserable for the Grayback Cop.

This 1908 headline from the *New York Times* reports on Opening Day at the Polo Grounds, which was held on Wednesday, April 22. Jack Norworth was not headlining in Manhattan during that week, and it is likely that he was using the time off to write new material for his upcoming out-of-town engagements.

Manhattan at Proctor's 125th and 5th Avenue Theatres and at the Colonial. On March 8 and March 15, both Sunday evenings (generally an off day or travel day for vaudevillians), Norworth appeared for one-night stands at the Gotham Theatre and the Dewey Theatre, respectively. Although these theaters were not on his regular circuit, Norworth likely used the evenings to try out new material.

On March 30 Norworth began a weeklong engagement (vaudeville engagements generally began with a Monday matinee and continued through Saturday; some theaters played seven days) at the Orpheum Theatre in Brooklyn. Then he was back in Manhattan at Hammerstein's Victoria for two weeks. Although his name appears in the theater's display ad for only the week of April 6, a New Jersey newspaper noted that Norworth's "Owl" song ("A Wise Old Owl") had been very popular at Hammerstein's the following week. After April 18 Norworth appears to have been without weeklong engagements for the remainder of the month.

In his later years Norworth, reminiscing to a newspaper reporter about "Take Me Out to the Ball Game," noted that an advertisement for a game at the Polo Grounds had inspired the song. Baseball's Opening Day that 1908 season was Tuesday, April 14, although the National League

Giants did not open at home at the Polo Grounds until the following Wednesday, April 22. If it was a Polo Grounds ad that inspired him to write his song, it is unlikely, given his schedule, that Norworth introduced the song at Hammerstein's.

Norworth did, however, join an illustrious cast of artists—"by far the greatest array of artists ever assembled in Brooklyn"—for a "colossal testimonial tendered to America's senior manager Leonard Grover, Sr." on Sunday, April 26, at Brooklyn's Grand Opera House, a date consistent with the oft-reported story that "Take Me Out to the Ball Game" had debuted in Brooklyn, a town known for its spirited vaudeville audiences.

Interestingly, in an April 19 display ad promoting the gala event, Nora Bayes is *not* listed as one of the performers. Nor is she listed in an accompanying news story about the benefit. The following week (April 26), however, her name had been added to the "greatest array of artists." Recall that a *Philadelphia Inquirer* story from October 1908 had discussed the June marriage of Bayes and Norworth and noted that Norworth had been retained earlier in the year to write songs for Bayes. Could "Take Me Out to the Ball Game" have been one of those songs?

The oft-repeated story of the song's 1908 Brooklyn debut places it at the Amphion Theatre, known throughout the 1890s for legitimate plays, not vaudeville, although under the management of William T. Grover, the son of Leonard Grover, the Amphion did feature vaudeville for several years until 1906. By late 1906 the theater had been acquired by Charles E. Blaney and renamed Blaney's Theatre (a 1908 Brooklyn business directory shows the same address, 439 Bedford Avenue, for both theaters, and newspaper display ads show that Mr. Blaney briefly called his theater Blaney's Amphion Theatre in early November 1906), and it was again featuring plays. By mid-November 1906, display ads for the Amphion Theatre no longer appeared in the *Brooklyn Daily Eagle*, although weekly ads for Blaney's Theatre did appear.

According to advertisements in the *Brooklyn Daily Eagle*, Norworth, in the earliest years of his career at the turn of the century, was a regular performer at several of Brooklyn's other theaters, including Hyde and Behman's (a "temple of variety"), the Brooklyn Music Hall, the Novelty, and the Gayety, but there is no evidence that he ever appeared at the

As shown here in the *Brooklyn Daily Eagle*, Jack Norworth and Nora Bayes joined
an illustrous cast in Brooklyn on Sunday, April 26, 1908, for a "colossal testimonial" to veteran playwright, theatrical manager, and operatic impresario
Leonard Grover. Sunday traditionally was a day off or a travel day for vaudevillians. Weeklong vaudeville engagements began with a Monday matinee.
Vaudeville theaters often presented concerts or benefits to draw the crowds in
on Sundays.

Amphion. By 1908 not only had Norworth hit the big time in vaudeville,
but Blaney's was featuring, most notably, plays starring "Brooklyn's
Favorite Comedienne," Cecil Spooner (whom Blaney married in 1909),
and her stock company. Beginning on April 20, 1908, Miss Spooner was
booked for three weeks at Blaney's Theatre with three different stage
productions, which makes it appear all the more unlikely that Norworth
was performing there in the weeks after the baseball season began.

A story in the *Brooklyn Daily Eagle* on April 19, 1908, notes that plans
were under way for a monster benefit to be tendered to the business staff
of Blaney's Amphion Theatre (indicating that the theater might still have
been known to local theatergoers as the Amphion) on Sunday evening,
May 17. Organizers were arranging a "big vaudeville bill." Might Norworth
have performed at that benefit and introduced "Take Me Out to the Ball
Game" that mid-May evening at Blaney's Amphion Theatre?

This 1906 *Brooklyn Daily Eagle* display ad for the big-time Orpheum Theatre in Brooklyn shows that Jack Norworth was already a star by the time "Take Me Out to the Ball Game" was published. It is unlikely that he would have returned to smaller venues after hitting the big-time.

From May 11 to May 16 Norworth was headlining at the Temple Theatre in Detroit (the manager's report noted that although his "new material was not as good as that he presented last year," Jack was "still quite a favorite here and is going very good") and was due to continue on to Pittsburgh the following week, although he cancelled that engagement due to illness and returned to New York. If, as it appears, he fulfilled his obligation in Detroit, could Norworth have been back in New York by the evening of Sunday, May 17?

Even if he had returned to New York, given the song's May 2 copyright date and the May copyright of George M. Cohan's coattail song, as well as the report in the May 9 issue of *Variety* that noted the similarity between

BASE BALL
NATIONAL LEAGUE
POLO GROUNDS
NEW YORK and BROOKLYN
April 22, 23, 24, 25.

A *New York Times* ad such as this one in 1908 might have inspired Jack Norworth to write "Take Me Out to the Ball Game."

the two songs, it is unlikely that "Take Me Out to the Ball Game" was introduced at Blaney's Amphion as late as May 17, and it is unlikely that Norworth even performed at that benefit.

He was, however, one of the prominent artists on the bill for a monster benefit at Keeney's, Brooklyn's "popular home of refined vaudeville," for Thursday evening, May 21. It is possible that Norworth, who had been a regular at Keeney's as he worked his way up the vaudeville ladder, sang his baseball song that evening, although the late May date again suggests that the song probably was not introduced that evening.

The date of the Brooklyn Grand Opera House event, April 26, is also consistent with Norworth's specific recollection that a Polo Grounds advertisement had inspired the writing of "Take Me Out to the Ball Game." That being the case, the song would likely have been written after April 22, Opening Day at the National League Polo Grounds; introduced within days, during Norworth and Bayes's appearance at the Grand Opera House gala; and copyrighted within a week after that. This timetable certainly is consistent with Tin Pan Alley's reputation for "rapid-fire songwriting" and for delivering songs from conception to sheet music within mere days. Just who sang the song, Norworth or Bayes (or both together), has probably been lost to history.

Incidentally, not too many months earlier, in December 1907, *Variety* had noted Tin Pan Alley's tendencies for rapid-fire songwriting when it reported that Norworth, appearing in Boston and in need of a new song

Brooklyn's Grand Opera House, located at Elm Place near Fulton Street, likely was the place where Jack Norworth and/or Nora Bayes introduced "Take Me Out to the Ball Game" in April 1908. (Brooklyn Public Library—Brooklyn Collection.)

to spruce up his act, had phoned Von Tilzer, who hummed a new tune over the phone. Norworth memorized the tune and within minutes had written lyrics. He phoned Von Tilzer again and sang the song back to him. The song was performed that evening with full orchestration.)

After Norworth's appearance at Brooklyn's Grand Opera House on April 26, he was again without a weeklong engagement, but he was on the road, probably by week's end, traveling to Rochester, New York, where he began an engagement at Cook's Opera House on May 4 to close out the vaudeville season. He continued on to Detroit. It is likely that he had used the previous several weeks of "leisure time" to write new songs (as he had earlier in the year, according to *Variety*) and to spruce up his act for his out-of-town performances. Factoring in the two days that were allotted for travel between engagements, Norworth may have left Manhattan by May 2, the very day his song was submitted for copyright.

The instant success of "Take Me Out to the Ball Game" was nudged along by Von Tilzer, who added "The Sensational Base Ball Song" to the title on the published sheet music (there were at least twelve versions of the sheet music issued in 1908, including one with a picture of Norworth and another with a picture of Bayes) and commissioned the illustrated song slides that plugged the song between film reels at nickelodeons.

For its "Take Me Out to the Ball Game" slides, DeWitt C. Wheeler hired models and chose the Polo Grounds as a backdrop for the song. A title slide depicted the sheet music cover. Additional slides told the story of Katie Casey, and a final slide, with the words to the catchy chorus, encouraged the audience to sing along. It wasn't long before "the sensational baseball song" was indeed everyone's favorite.

Despite George M. Cohan's taking every opportunity to advertise his song, and having the money to do so, his Broadway stature did not guarantee that "Take Your Girl to the Ball Game" would be a hit. Some years after the footlights had dimmed for both Norworth and Cohan, Norworth is said to have told an interviewer that he was secretly pleased that the Cohan song had not done as well as his own. Or so the story goes.

Nor had the song "Base Ball," the "home-run hit" by Roger Lewis

New York lantern slide maker DeWitt C. Wheeler was commissioned by the York Music Company to make song slides for "Take Me Out to the Ball Game." The illustrated slides told the story of Katie Casey's day at the ballpark. (National Baseball Hall of Fame Library, Cooperstown, New York.)

and Al Brown, done as well as Norworth's. Published by the Thompson Music Company of Chicago in May 1908, the song was advertised as the "newest, best and most original novelty song of the National Game" and was a clear attempt to capitalize on the momentum of the Norworth and Cohan songs. "Base Ball" made little, if any, impression on the public. Nor did another Al Brown song, "I Want to Go to the Ball Game," published in 1909.

One of the early editions of sheet music for "Take Me Out to the Ball Game" featured Jack Norworth on the cover. Other stars of the era, including Nora Bayes, also graced sheet music covers, which became collectible souvenirs in their day, especially if they were autographed. In 1936 the song's subtitle was changed to "The Famous Baseball Song," and in 1949 it was changed again to "The Official Baseball Song." (National Baseball Hall of Fame Library, Cooperstown, New York.)

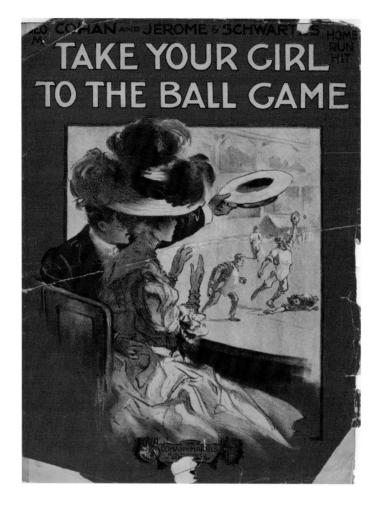

George M. Cohan's "Take Your Girl to the Ball Game" didn't have the public appeal that Norworth's song did, despite Cohan's avalanche of advertising and unrivalled reputation for turning out hits. Cohan tried to appeal to the "emerging woman" with a charming, romantic sheet music cover. (The Lester S. Levy Collection of Sheet Music, Special Collections, Sheridan Libraries, The Johns Hopkins University.)

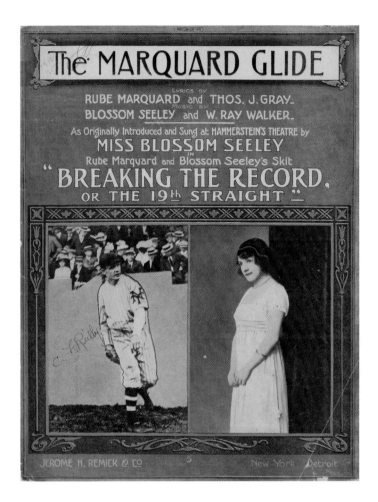

Richard William "Rube" Marquard was one of many baseball stars who performed on the vaudeville stage in the off-season, but not every baseball vaudevillian could boast his own song, "The Marquard Glide." Rube Marquard glided his way across the stage, as Blossom Seeley, who later became Mrs. Marquard, sang the 1912 song. A glide was a type of waltz with a smooth gliding step. (The Lester S. Levy Collection of Sheet Music, Special Collections, Sheridan Libraries, The Johns Hopkins University.)

One of the earliest pieces of baseball sheet music, the "Live Oak Polka," written in 1860 for piano, was dedicated to the Live Oak Base Ball Club of Rochester, New York. The polka was a fast dance consisting of a hop followed by three small steps. Like other sheet music covers, the cover of "Live Oak Polka" is cherished for its beautiful color and graphics, including American symbols. (The Lester S. Levy Collection of Sheet Music, Special Collections, Sheridan Libraries, The Johns Hopkins University.)

After his success with "Take Me Out to the Ball Game," Albert von Tilzer tried again with "Back to the Bleachers for Mine." The words to this 1910 waltz song hint at Von Tilzer's earlier baseball hit. (The Lester S. Levy Collection of Sheet Music, Special Collections, Sheridan Libraries, The Johns Hopkins University.)

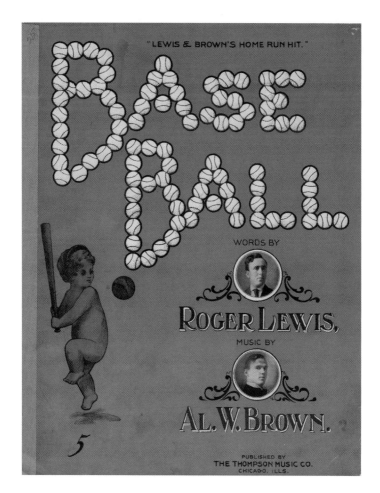

On the coattails of "Take Me Out to the Ball Game" and "Take Your Girl to the Ball Game," Roger Lewis and Al Brown published "Base Ball" in May 1908. They dedicated their "home-run hit" to the baseball fans. The song met with little success, despite the hype surrounding the Norworth and Cohan songs and the fact that the 1908 baseball season was one of the most exciting of all time. (The Lester S. Levy Collection of Sheet Music, Special Collections, Sheridan Libraries, The Johns Hopkins University.)

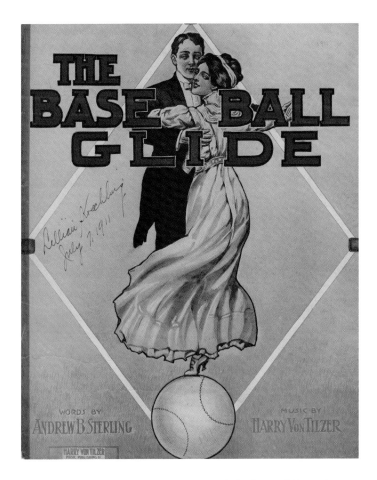

Harry von Tilzer, known as the "man who launched a thousand hits," whose own compositions included "Wait 'Till the Sun Shines, Nellie" and "I Want a Girl," was unable to launch a baseball hit of his own with "The Base Ball Glide" in 1911. The sheet music cover is notable for its lovely graphics and its themes of courtship and dancing. (The Lester S. Levy Collection of Sheet Music, Special Collections, Sheridan Libraries, The Johns Hopkins University.)

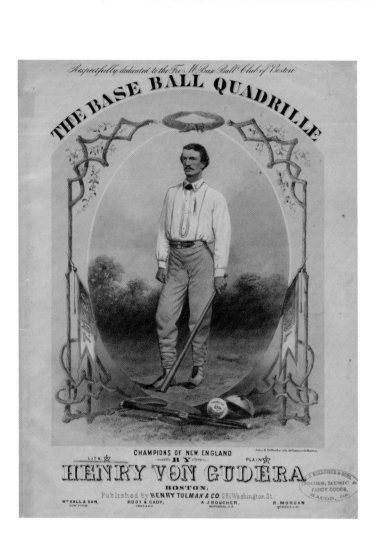

This very early and very beautiful piece of baseball sheet music, published in 1867, featured nuanced color and eye-catching typography and design. A quadrille was a popular ballroom dance of the nineteenth century, a square dance of French origin for four couples. (The Lester S. Levy Collection of Sheet Music, Special Collections, Sheridan Libraries, The Johns Hopkins University.)

Early baseball sheet music attracted buyers with charming pastoral scenes that evoked nostalgia for a time that was quickly disappearing during America's industrial age. This 1867 song, "Base Ball Polka," was dedicated to "the fraternity." (The Lester S. Levy Collection of Sheet Music, Special Collections, Sheridan Libraries, The Johns Hopkins University.)

Jack Norworth and Nora Bayes, pictured on the cover of "Shine On, Harvest Moon," composed the song for the Ziegfeld Follies of 1908. The Follies of 1908 opened on June 15 at the Jardin de Paris (atop the New York Theatre) and moved to the New York Theatre on September 7. The show closed on September 26 after 120 performances. Previous commitments kept Norworth from joining the Follies until September. No doubt the approach of autumn was the inspiration for this song. (The Lester S. Levy Collection of Sheet Music, Special Collections, Sheridan Libraries, The Johns Hopkins University.)

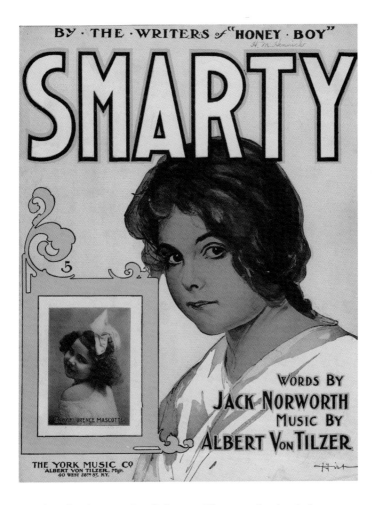

In early 1908 Jack Norworth and Albert von Tilzer were already enjoying success with their latest hit, "Smarty." A few weeks later they published their sensational baseball song, "Take Me Out to the Ball Game." (The Lester S. Levy Collection of Sheet Music, Special Collections, Sheridan Libraries, The Johns Hopkins University.)

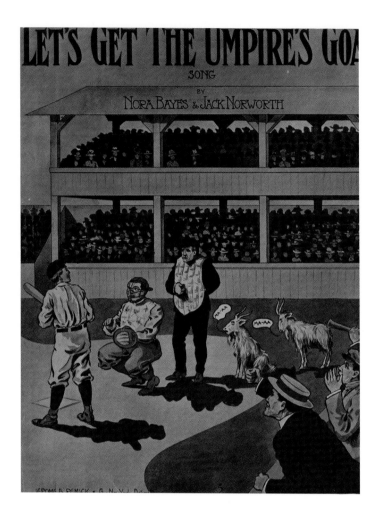

Jack Norworth and Nora Bayes were back in 1909 for Florenz Ziegfeld's new-est Follies production, which opened June 14 and for which they wrote "Let's Get the Umpire's Goat." The couple departed the show in early July, but the show continued until August 7, closing after sixty-four performances. Little has changed in the century since the song was written. Fans still try to annoy or an-ger the umpire—to get his goat. (The Lester S. Levy Collection of Sheet Music, Special Collections, Sheridan Libraries, The Johns Hopkins University.)

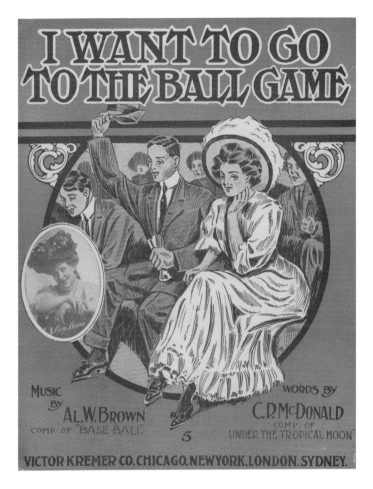

Written in a waltz tempo by Al Brown (who a year earlier had hoped to capitalize on the success of "Take Me Out to the Ball Game" with his own song, "Base Ball"), this 1909 song, "I Want to Go to the Ball Game," was also unable to capture the public's fancy. The sheet music cover graphics are reminiscent of those for "Take Your Girl to the Ball Game," and the song lyrics hint of "Take Me Out to the Ball Game." (The Lester S. Levy Collection of Sheet Music, Special Collections, Sheridan Libraries, The Johns Hopkins University.)

Dedicated to the Mercantile Base Ball Club of Philadelphia, this 1861 piano composition, "Home Run Quick Step," has a fine lithographic cover typical of the earliest baseball songs. A quick step is a march in the rhythm of quick time—with spirit. (The Lester S. Levy Collection of Sheet Music, Special Collections, Sheridan Libraries, The Johns Hopkins University.)

In this "Take Me Out to the Ball Game" song slide, Katie Casey asks her beau to take her to the game. (National Baseball Hall of Fame Library, Cooperstown, New York.

No sooner had "Take Me Out to the Ball Game" become a hit with the public than the major phonograph companies began recording the song. Thirty years earlier, in 1877, Thomas Edison had invented the tin foil "phonograph," his trade name for a machine that recorded and produced sound. The first recordings were made by a vibrating stylus that incised the voice in vertical grooves on strips of tin foil wrapped around a four-inch-diameter cylinder. By 1888 cylinders were smaller, two inches in diameter, and made of a soft, fragile brownish wax material. Until 1894 all recordings had been made on cylinders; by 1912 discs had replaced cylinders.

To record their songs, performers stood in the midst of phonographs

In this song slide, Katie Casey "roots, roots, roots for the home team."
(National Baseball Hall of Fame Library, Cooperstown, New York.)

with funnel-shaped horns and sang in a clear, strong voice. High volume
was needed to cause the cutting stylus to vibrate and indent the blank
cylinders. Before duplicating methods were invented, all-day sessions
of take after take after take of the song were needed to make multiple
recordings. Each cylinder was, in a sense, an original recording.

Edison improved upon his phonograph (and began working on other
projects, including moving pictures, which he first demonstrated in
1891; in 1898 he produced a motion picture of a baseball game), and
in 1902 he developed the "Edison Gold-Moulded Records" process, a
method for duplicating cylinders from wax masters. Commercially successful for the first decade of the twentieth century, Edison cylinders,

EDISON STANDARD PHONOGRAPH.
DECORATED HORN

Thomas Edison's 1908 phonograph is depicted here with a fancy horn.
(Edison National Historic Site, National Park Service, U.S. Department
of the Interior.)

with a playing time of two minutes, enabled hundreds of the decade's
hit songs, instrumentals, ethnic comedy skits, and vaudeville acts to
be played on phonographs in homes and in vaudeville houses, nickelodeons, and arcades.

While Edison was perfecting his cylinder in his Menlo Park, New
Jersey, laboratory, Emile Berliner, a German immigrant who had settled
in Washington, DC, was experimenting with imprinted grooves on flat
zinc discs—records—that proved in time to be easier to handle and store,
more durable, and less expensive, and had a longer playing time than
cylinders. Discs eventually doomed the cylinder. Granted patents for his
"Gram-o-phone" in 1887 and 1888, Berliner eventually sold the rights
to his gramophone company to the Victor Talking Machine Company,
one of the major recording labels of the day.

It was on a two-minute Edison wax cylinder that one of the earliest
known recordings of "Take Me Out to the Ball Game" was made by

The earliest recordings, made on Edison wax cylinders, were often sold door-to-door by a salesman with a company horse and wagon. (Edison National Historic Site, National Park Service, United States Department of the Interior.)

vaudevillian Edward Meeker in September 1908. Meeker, a baritone and one of the Edison Minstrels (a studio recording group) is perhaps best known to music aficionados for making the spoken introductions (there was no space for a label on a cylinder) for hundreds of Edison cylinders, including "Take Me Out to the Ball Game."

According to the Columbia discography, tenor Harvey Hindermyer, another session singer, recorded the song with an orchestra on a single-faced Columbia Phonograph Company record in August 1908.

The Haydn Quartet, a popular turn-of-the-century harmony quartet, recorded "Take Me Out to the Ball Game" (without Billy Murray) on a single-faced disc for Victor on September 9, 1908—the earliest recording of the song in the Victor discography. A year later the Victor Orchestra included the song in an instrumental medley recorded on September 29, 1909. The song was not recorded again on the Victor label until 1929.

Edison's Gold-Moulded process was developed in 1902. Hundreds of the era's vaudeville skits and songs were recorded on wax cylinders. Few performers realized that the recordings, which Americans could enjoy in the comfort of their own living rooms, would have an impact on theater attendance. (Edison National Historic Site, National Park Service, United States Department of the Interior.)

In September 1908 Edison studio musician Edward Meeker, shown here, made one of the earliest known recordings of "Take Me Out to the Ball Game" on a two-minute wax cylinder. (Edison National Historic Site, National Park Service, United States Department of the Interior.)

Another of the first recordings of "Take Me Out to the Ball Game," was that by the Haydn Quartet, a popular turn-of-the-century harmony group, who recorded the song for Victor in 1908. (Archeophone Records Collection.)

Neither Jack Norworth nor Nora Bayes ever recorded the song. However, in 1940 a recording by Albert von Tilzer was made at a live concert celebrating the conclusion of the Golden Gate International Exposition.

In the years following the first recordings of "Take Me Out to the Ball Game," a number of well-known performers, including the Andrews Sisters, Bing Crosby, and the Boston Pops Orchestra, recorded the song. The Marx Brothers got laughs with the song when they slipped it into a scene from *A Night at the Opera*. Gene Kelly and Frank Sinatra sang the 1927 "Nellie Kelly" version for the 1949 MGM movie musical *Take Me Out to the Ball Game*, which starred Kelly and Sinatra as turn-of-the-century ballplayers who perform vaudeville during the off-season.

By 1949 the sheet music subtitle, which had changed from "The Sensational Base Ball Song" to "The Famous Baseball Song" when the copyright was renewed in 1936, had changed again to "The Official Baseball Song." If baseball had long ago been recognized as the national pastime, it now finally had an official song to reflect its status.

Whereas most early baseball songs had a brief life, their sheet music having but one printing before the songs were forgotten, "Take Me Out to the Ball Game" proved the exception. No other baseball song achieved the popularity that it retained over time, although there are relatively few early recordings in the early discographies. In 1955 *Variety*, the magazine founded fifty years earlier to celebrate and promote vaudeville, named the song one of the ten greatest popular songs of the previous half-century.

There was still one chapter to be written in the story of the sensational baseball song, however. Against the backdrop of Chicago's Comiskey Park in 1976, the bicentennial of the United States, White Sox owner and marketing genius Bill Veeck Jr.—the Benjamin Franklin Keith of baseball—would elevate "Take Me Out to the Ball Game" to more than a popular song, to more than baseball's official song. With the cooperation of broadcaster Harry Caray, Bill Veeck would make the song an anthem and the singing of the song during the seventh-inning stretch a time-honored baseball tradition.

7

Let Me Hear You Good and Loud . . . A-one, A-two, A-three

Baseball's unique possession, the real source of our strength, is the fan's memory of the times his daddy took him to the game to see the great players of his youth. Whether he remembers it or not, the excitement of those hours, the step they represented in his own growth and the part those afternoons—even one afternoon—played in his relationship with his own father is bound up in his feeling toward the local ball club and toward the game. When he takes his own son to the game, as his father once took him, there is a spanning of the generations that is warm and rich, and—if I may use the word—lovely.   BILL VEECK

Throughout the heyday of his career, until the late 1920s, whenever a newspaper story appeared about Norworth's "jaunty air," his "knack for naturalness," or his ability to deliver "perfect entertainment," it did not neglect to mention that among his long list of songs of the "whistling and popular variety" was "Take Me Out to the Ball Game." However, the song was never singled out as anything more or less than his many other hits—hits that included "Honey Boy," "Over on the Jersey Side," "Dolly Dear," "I'm Glad I'm a Boy and I'm Glad I'm a Girl," and "Shine On, Harvest Moon."

In the September 1957 issue of *Hobbies* magazine, the story about the recordings of Jack Norworth is interesting for what it doesn't say. Reference is made to "Take Me Out to the Ball Game" being rated by the American Society of Composers, Authors and Publishers as an American folk song—not baseball's official song but simply an American folk song.

Another curious omission is what old-time vaudevillian Joe Laurie Jr.'s landmark reminiscence, *Vaudeville: From the Honky-tonks to the Palace*, doesn't say. Laurie's chatty, affectionate look back on the heyday of vaudeville, published in 1953, includes numerous references to Norworth and Bayes as well as several pages about baseball, but it never mentions "Take Me Out to the Ball Game." Laurie certainly would have known Norworth, who was older by thirteen years. Both men were members of the Lamb's Theatre Club in New York for twenty-five years.

There is no doubt that the song was popular in its day (thanks to the baseball mania that was sweeping the country as well as to Norworth's popularity), having gone through numerous sheet music printings in 1908 and one recording by each of the four major recording companies— Edison, Victor, Zonophone, and Columbia—while remaining a favorite even as vaudeville declined in the 1930s. Chances are the sunny "Take Me Out to the Ball Game" would have continued to be durable—one of those popular, easily recognizable Tin Pan Alley "folk" songs like "Bill Bailey," "Daisy Bell," or "Let Me Call You Sweetheart" that is passed down through the generations, a few words and snippets of tune known by everyone. But two baseball legends—Harry Caray, a future Ford Frick Award-winning broadcaster, and future Hall of Fame team owner and promoter, Bill Veeck Jr.—two gentlemen who had a great respect for one another, had other plans for the song, although they probably did not imagine that their "great gag" would elevate "Take Me Out to the Ball Game" to anthem status and make singing the song during the seventh-inning stretch a time-honored baseball tradition. The team of Bill Veeck and Harry Caray gave the song something that it had not achieved in its previous seven decades. They gave the song—its chorus, at least— universality and immortality. They made it baseball's anthem.

Harry Caray was born Harry Carabina in St. Louis in 1914, the same year that Veeck was born. After flunking an army physical, he played a little semiprofessional baseball and then embarked on a career in radio broadcasting, only to be told by management that his name sounded "too foreign." Like so many ethnic vaudevillians of a generation earlier, he changed his birth name—to Harry Caray. The name, though with a different spelling, was a familiar one to moviegoers of the day.

Holy Cow! Legendary baseball broadcaster Harry Caray teamed up with White Sox owner Bill Veeck Jr. to make the singing of "Take Me Out to the Ball Game" a seventh-inning stretch tradition. (Museum of Broadcast Communications, PH 02012.)

Bill Veeck Jr. son of former Chicago Cubs president Bill Veeck, is shown here outside Comiskey Park. As a kid the younger Bill Veeck sold hot dogs and peanuts at Wrigley Field when his dad was club president. (Courtesy Rucker Archive/Transcendental Graphics.)

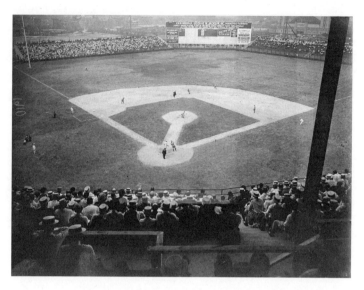

A bird's-eye view from behind the plate at the new Comiskey Park, home of the White Sox, 1910. (Chicago History Museum, SDN-008839.)

That "other" Harry Carey, born Henry DeWitt Carey in the Bronx in 1878 and the son of a New York judge, became a popular silent film cowboy star during the 1910s and 1920s. After a stint in vaudeville, Carey found a second career in talking pictures and continued to perform until his death in 1947. By coincidence (or perhaps not), baseball connects the two Harrys. Harry Carey, the actor, starred as aging catcher Tom Munson in the 1927 MGM silent film *Slide, Kelly, Slide,* which featured a cameo appearance by the New York Giants outfielder Mike Donlin, who moonlighted, even during his playing days, on the vaudeville stage. Perhaps this legacy is what inspired Harry Carabina to change his name to Harry Caray. Or perhaps the rookie broadcaster's name change was inspired by the "sensational song hit" "Carrie Marry Harry," published by the York Music Company in 1909, which had lyrics written by Junie McCree and music by none other than Albert von Tilzer!

Whatever his inspiration, in 1945 Harry Carabina began his fifty-three-year, 8,300-game career as baseball announcer and storyteller

Two baseball legends, Charles Comiskey (left), owner of the American League Chicago White Sox, and Bill Veeck Sr., president of the National League Chicago Cubs, are shown here in 1920. Nearly forty years later Veeck's son was part of a group of investors that wrested control of the White Sox from the Comiskey family. (Chicago History Museum, SDN-062205.)

Harry Caray as the voice of his hometown Cardinals. By 1970 he had gone west to broadcast for the Oakland Athletics. A year later Caray was in Chicago, at Comiskey Park, where he was the voice of the White Sox until 1981.

The White Sox had moved to Chicago from St. Paul in 1900, and they played during their first decade at South Side Park, an old cricket field on which Charles Comiskey had built a wooden grandstand. On July 1, 1910, the new Comiskey Park opened, and by 1927 an outfield upper deck had been added to accommodate an additional twenty-three thousand fans.

In December 1958 a group of investors, which included the maverick

Bill Veeck Jr. wrested control of the White Sox from the Comiskey family. Like vaudevillians of a generation or two earlier, Veeck, a Chicago native, had grown up in the family business. The son of former Chicago Cubs president Bill Veeck, Sr., the junior Veeck had spent his childhood selling peanuts and hot dogs at the Cubs' Wrigley Field, the first team, interestingly, to play organ music (in 1941) in the ballpark. By 1946 he had bought his first professional Major League team, the Cleveland Indians. It was during his tenure with the Indians that Veeck, in 1947, signed Larry Doby, the first African American to play in the American League and the second African American to play Major League baseball. Jackie Robinson had broken the color barrier earlier in the season when he signed with the National League Dodgers.

But Veeck was and would always be more than a team owner. He prided himself on being a regular guy who seemed to understand instinctively the needs and wants of fans. It was Veeck's simple belief that a team owner should first take care of the fans, and to that end he introduced the fun and games, like fireworks, that brought fans through the turnstyles and provided a memorable experience at the ballpark—even for those who might be indifferent to baseball.

By 1951, after selling the Indians, Veeck had bought the St. Louis Browns, a team that had become an American League franchise in 1901. It was in St. Louis that Veeck introduced Grandstand Managers' Day, for which fans were given large placards marked "YES" or "NO" so that they could express their approval or disapproval of the manager's game strategy. (In an interesting parallel, Jack Norworth occasionally left it to the audience to decide if the act that followed him would be a dramatic skit, a musical comedy skit, a saxophone duet, or an acrobat.) Veeck's fun, while it did indeed draw fans, annoyed his fellow team owners. Forced to sell the team in 1953, Veeck was back in baseball five years later as owner of the White Sox.

Health problems in 1961 forced Veeck to sell his interest in the team to his business associate, but by December of 1975 he was again the team's owner. The next season, the year of the U.S. Bicentennial, the impresario Veeck enlisted broadcaster Harry Caray in another plan for fun and games, an idea that proved to be brilliant and legendary: Caray would lead the crowd in the singing of "Take Me Out to the Ball Game" during the seventh-inning stretch.

The time-honored ritual of standing up and stretching before the hometown team comes to bat in the seventh inning is recognized by baseball historians as dating to 1869, the year the first professional team, Harry Wright's Cincinnati Red Stockings, was formed. In a letter to a friend, Wright noted that the "spectators all arise between halves of the seventh inning, extend their legs and arms and sometimes walk about. In so doing they enjoy the relief afforded by relaxation from a long posture upon hard benches."

Before Harry Wright's letter came to light, there were several other explanations for the seventh-inning stretch tradition. Among them was the sacred number theory. For those who subscribe to the notion that the power and spiritual energy of numbers operate subconsciously in everyone, the number seven—lucky seven—is replete with magic and mystery. Because it is also the number of renewal, it seemed only natural that fans of a game that is so dominated by numbers would renew themselves with a stretch in the seventh inning.

Then there was Brother Jasper, Manhattan College's Prefect of Discipline, who introduced baseball to the school. From 1863 to 1894, Brother Jasper managed the team and supervised the student fans. On one particularly hot and humid day in the late 1880s, while Manhattan College was playing against a semiprofessional team, Brother Jasper noticed that the fans were becoming restless by the seventh inning. He called for a pause in the action and directed the spectators to stand up and stretch, an interlude so well received that Brother Jasper made it a part of every game. The tradition was said to have spread to the professional leagues when the college played exhibition games against the New York Giants at the Polo Grounds during the 1890s.

Still others attribute the seventh-inning stretch to President Taft, who is said to have unwittingly begun the custom when he was uncomfortable in his seat and rose to stretch his legs. The crowd, believing that the president was leaving the game, rose from their seats in a show of respect, only to sit back down when the president did too. President

Some historians argue that this man—Joseph Brennan, Brother Jasper of
Mary—"invented" the seventh-inning-stretch tradition in the late nineteenth
century when he managed the Manhattan College baseball team. (Photograph
courtesy of the De La Salle Christian Brothers Archives of the New York
District.)

Taft, by the way, is said to have been the first president to throw out the first ball on Opening Day (in 1909).

If its beginning, like baseball's beginning, is cloaked in a bit of mystery, the seventh-inning stretch was a well-established custom by the time Harry Caray arrived on Chicago's South Side in 1971. To amuse himself during commercial breaks between innings, Caray routinely stood up in the booth and sang "Take Me Out to the Ball Game," the only song, he was fond of saying, to which he knew the words. One day in 1976 Bill Veeck heard Caray singing and convinced him that if they opened the microphone in the broadcast booth the fans would be able to hear Caray and would spontaneously sing along.

The prevailing notion that Veeck secretly installed a microphone in the booth and recorded Caray against his knowledge or will is, says Veeck's son Mike, himself a team owner and apostle of fun, "preposterous." Although initially reluctant to sing publicly, for fear that the fans might make fun of his voice, Caray was eventually convinced by Veeck that his singing would make everyone else brave and that the fans would all join in. "That was the great allure," says Mike Veeck. "My father knew that the guy sitting in left field would think that he could sing it just as well."

Caray's son, the late Atlanta Braves broadcaster Skip Caray, tells the same story. "Dad always felt (and I agree) that the reason the whole thing was successful was because he had such a lousy voice that the fans had nothing to lose by singing along. They couldn't have sung it any worse!"

Bill Veeck, the self-proclaimed "regular guy" who seemed always to know what the fans wanted, had knocked another one out of the park. Caray, the "people's announcer," began leading the crowd—"Let me hear you good and loud, a-one, a-two, a-three"—in the singing of "Take Me Out to the Ball Game" during every seventh-inning stretch. Leaning out of his broadcast booth and swinging his microphone in time with the music, Caray, who, despite his "lousy voice," loved music and counted Frank Sinatra and Nat King Cole among his friends, encouraged the crowd to join in, just as vaudeville and nickelodeon audiences seventy years earlier had been encouraged by illustrated song slides to join in.

In 1981, when Caray left the White Sox, he took the seventh-inning stretch tradition of singing "Take Me Out to the Ball Game" with him across town to Wrigley Field and the Chicago Cubs, the team for which Bill Veeck Jr. had sold peanuts and hot dogs when his father was club president. At Wrigley Field, Caray encouraged the crowd to root, root, root for the Cubbies. Veeck, who had sold the White Sox before the 1981 season, was often out in the bleachers at Wrigley, watching the game with all the other regular folks—the average Joes—and singing along with Harry Caray. In 1991, when Veeck was elected to the Hall of Fame, his induction plaque noted that he was "a champion of the little guy."

When Caray died in 1998, ninety years after "Take Me Out to the Ball Game" was written, the tradition of root, root, rooting for the Cubbies continued, and it still continues, in his memory, with guest singers leading the crowd.

Coincidentally, the year the song was written, 1908, was the last year that the Cubs won the World Series, defeating the Detroit Tigers in a five-game series after winning the National League Championship in that decisive playoff game against the New York Giants on October 8, 1908.

8

Baseball as Vaudeville

We shall not cease from exploration, And the end of all our exploring will be to arrive where we started and know the place for the first time.   T. S. ELIOT

Over the years historians have often noted the "cross-fertilization" be-tween baseball and vaudeville. The song "Take Me Out to the Ball Game" and the MGM musical of the same title, which featured Gene Kelly and Frank Sinatra as baseball players who "play" vaudeville in the off-season in 1906, might be the best examples of that symbiosis, but by no means are they the only ones. In fact, the relationship between baseball and vaudeville began at least twenty years before Jack Norworth and Albert von Tilzer wrote "Take Me Out to the Ball Game," when the respected thespian DeWolf Hopper recited a "thrilling ode" at Wallack's Theatre on a hot August night in 1888.

That summer Hopper had a starring role in the McCaull Opera Company's production of Strauss's comic opera *Prince Methusalem*. On August 14 Wallack's Theatre hosted baseball night. The actors, who had been guests at the Polo Grounds that afternoon, reciprocated by invit-ing members of the New York Giants and Cap Anson's Chicago White Stockings to the evening performance, where the "nines" were among the large and enthusiastic audience. As a special treat for the baseball guests DeWolf, a self-proclaimed baseball "crank," offered a dramatic recitation of the poem "Casey at the Bat," which one reviewer said was "most uproariously received, particularly the ending thereof, which told in mock-heroic strain how the redoubtable Casey 'struck out.'"

"Casey at the Bat" had originally been published in June of 1888 in the

On August 15, 1888, the theater critic for the *New York Times* reviewed *Prince Methusalem*, during which its star, DeWolf Hopper, surprised his baseball audience by reciting a "thrilling ode," the poem *Casey at the Bat*. The poem had been published a few weeks earlier in the *San Francisco Daily Examiner*. It was written by *Harvard Lampoon* alumnus Ernest L. Thayer, who signed his name simply as "Phin."

"TEN THOUSAND EYES WERE ON HIM AS HE RUBBED HIS HANDS WITH DIRT"

"BUT THERE IS NO JOY IN MUDVILLE—MIGHTY CASEY HAS STRUCK OUT"

"WHENEVER HOPPER APPEARS BEFORE THE FOOTLIGHTS"

This early illustration of "Casey at the Bat" from the A. G. Spalding Collection of the New York Public Library immortalizes the mighty Casey striking out. (Photography Collection, Miriam and Ira D. Wallach Division of Art, Prints and Photographs, The New York Public Library, Astor, Lenox and Tilden Foundations.)

San Francisco Examiner. The poem, which tells the story of the Mudville nine, was written by *Harvard Lampoon* alumnus Ernest L. Thayer, who signed his poem simply "Phin." It received little attention in the newspaper but was clipped and given to DeWolf Hopper by a friend who was aware of the upcoming baseball evening at Wallack's. The reception for the poem that August evening was so favorable that Hopper made it a staple of his act, and over the next decade he recited it, by his account, ten thousand times.

By the time Jack Norworth and Albert von Tilzer were penning their "sensational baseball song" twenty years later, the relationship between baseball and vaudeville appeared to be well established. With ballplayers occupying special box seats, vaudeville houses often hosted benefit performances—Baseball Night—with proceeds going to charity. The stars of the diamond were often herded onto the stage to receive gifts and flowers from adoring fans. One vaudeville novelty act, the Green Brothers, introduced a baseball theme with their baseball bat juggling

Sparkling with Novelty and Pleasant Surprises

The baseball craze of the turn of the century found its way, in the form of novelty acts, onto many a vaudeville stage, as is shown here in an early, circa 1900, advertisement for the Green Brothers baseball bat juggling act. (Courtesy Rucker Archive/Transcendental Graphics.)

routine. Another, Power's Dancing Elephants (four elephants who played baseball with their trainer), was a favorite at the New York Hippodrome and eventually played the Palace. "Sporting Days" at the theater featured "real" baseball played on stage.

For his 1909 Follies, Flo Ziegfeld Jr. featured "America's Happiest Couple," Jack Norworth and Nora Bayes, singing their new baseball song, "Let's Get the Umpire's Goat." Also in the Follies program was another baseball number, "Come On, Play Ball with Me Dearie," during which a team of chorus girls, dressed in New York uniforms, played baseball on stage. Roasted peanuts, a staple at the ballpark, were also enjoyed in vaudeville theaters.

And as Gene Kelly and Frank Sinatra suggested by "burlesquing" on the big screen as Eddie O'Brien and Dennis Ryan, who, along with Nat Goldberg, turned double-play combinations—O'Brien-to-Ryan-to-Goldberg—for the fictitious Wolves (a spoof on the Tinker-Evers-Chance combination), it was also not unusual for real ballplayers to

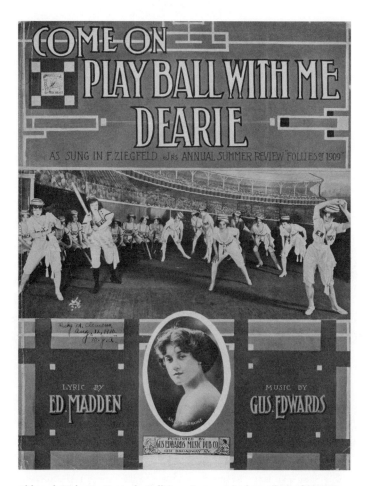

Although "Take Me Out to the Ball Game" was not in the 1908 Ziegfeld Follies program, Norworth and Bayes did write another baseball number, "Let's Get the Umpire's Goat," for the 1909 Follies. Bayes sang the song, and Norworth playcd an umpire in the skit. The program for the 1909 Follies also included the baseball song "Come On, Play Ball with Me Dearie." (The Lester S. Levy Collection of Sheet Music, Special Collections, Sheridan Libraries, The Johns Hopkins University.)

Like many athletes today, turn-of-the-century baseball stars often crossed over onto the theatrical stage. *A Runaway Colt* was written for baseball's Cap Anson, who starred in the production. (Courtesy Rucker Archive/Transcendental Graphics.)

The *New York Times* reviewed Cap Anson's performance in *A Runaway Colt* in Syracuse in November 1895.

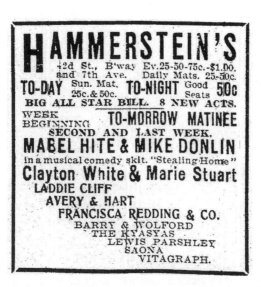

New York Giants star Mike Donlin and his wife, the beautiful actress Mabel
Hite, whom Donlin married in 1906, had their own vaudeville skit, *Stealing
Home*, which is advertised here in the *New York Times*. The show was Donlin's
first, although not his last, appearance behind the footlights. He later became
quite prominent in the motion picture industry.

try their hand at musical numbers and comedy skits on the vaudeville
stage.

Player-manager Adrian "Cap" Anson made his theatrical debut in
1895 in *A Runaway Colt*, a farce written expressly for Anson by Charles
H. Hoyt, who hoped to capitalize on the legendary "Anson's Colts" and
Anson's role as father figure to a team of young players. One theater
critic in Syracuse (the show also played on Broadway and in Brooklyn,
Chicago, and Minneapolis) noted that although Anson was "scarcely
an actor," he was "thoroughly in earnest."

Giants star Mike Donlin had his own one-act play, *Stealing Home*, in
which he starred with his stunning wife, Mabel Hite. After debuting
the skit at Hammerstein's in October 1908, the couple performed it at
big-time theaters from coast to coast during the next three winters.

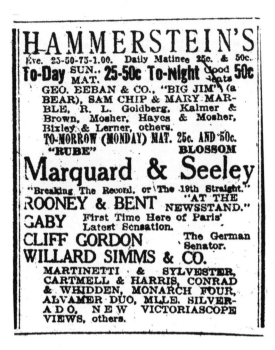

This *New York Times* ad features *Breaking the Record*, a vaudeville skit in which Hall of Fame pitcher Richard William "Rube" Marquard danced to his own song, "The Marquard Glide."

Another Giants star, pitcher Richard William "Rube" Marquard, who made his baseball debut in 1908, also left his mark on vaudeville. "The Marquard Glide," written by Marquard and Miss Blossom Seeley (who later became his wife), was introduced and sung by Seeley at Hammerstein's Theatre in 1912 during their skit, *Breaking the Record, or the 19th Straight*, which commemorated Marquard's 1912 nineteen-game winning streak.

The great Honus "Hans" Wagner, calling himself a has-been, considered retirement after the 1908 season to devote more time to his investments in circus enterprises. He was, of course, back in uniform for the Pirates in 1909 and continued to play until 1917.

Then there was the curious tale of Jack Dillon, a former catcher for a Jersey City team, who, after his playing days were over, starred in vaudeville with his trick dog, who earned a weekly wage of twenty-five dollars, *twice* the wage of the average worker in 1908. Dillon made headlines when, after his dog was killed by an automobile, he sued the car's driver for five hundred dollars!

If ballplayers were often spotted at the vaudeville theater, so too were the stars of Broadway and vaudeville regular rooters at the ballpark. In April 1908 *Variety* magazine noted that Opening Day at the American League grounds had broken up rehearsals for an Actor's Union benefit. The report noted that the director was "deeply puzzled" when so many members of the cast called, "begging off on a wide variety of excuses."

By mid-May, *Variety* was reporting that baseball enthusiasts were agitating to form a league of nines made up of employees from Greater New York vaudeville theaters.

DeWolf Hopper and George M. Cohan were said to have had their own private box at the Polo Grounds from which they serenaded Giants manager John McGraw. Billy Murray, "the Denver Nightingale," an immensely popular recording artist of the early phonograph era and the preeminent interpreter of George M. Cohan songs, was a die-hard Yankees (Highlanders) fan, often donning a uniform and playing for the team in exhibition games.

Theater folks held regular field days at the ballpark, raising money for charitable causes. On July 17, 1908, at an all-star, open-air carnival for charity, Louise Dresser umpired a baseball game featuring a team of Cohan's Yankee Doodles! A year later Nora Bayes and Jack Norworth entertained spectators at the New York Highlanders' American League park during a charitable event in aid of the Newsboys' Home. (Mike Donlin refereed a pie-eating contest at the same event!)

And there were, of course, the songs written about the game and its marquee players (who often posed for the cover of the sheet music), songs that were plugged with illustrated slides made at the National and American League ballparks.

The relationship between baseball and vaudeville, however, reached far beyond any particular performance or individual. From the start, from the very first inning, baseball and vaudeville had shared a culture, an ethos.

Both amusements offered a vicarious thrill for audiences, an escape from the tedium of daily life. Both brought people of vastly different ethnic backgrounds together as a community for a shared, intimate experience during which a kind of alchemy happened, a transmutation from stranger to friend. Vaudeville audiences and baseball fans loyally followed the careers of their favorites, welcoming them when they came to town (though there were always those "fans" who could make life on the road hellish for vaudevillians as well as ballplayers). In turn, vaudeville houses and baseball teams gave small towns and cities a cultural identity and elevated their star performers, like Giants' hurler Christy "Matty" Mathewson and Broadway's George M. Cohan, to that status of American cultural icon.

Both types of entertainment employed a "circuit" and a "player development" system. Small vaudeville houses were the equivalent of baseball's farm system, and every vaudevillian, like every Minor League ballplayer, aspired to the big time. Even the new generation of concrete and steel ballparks, which called themselves "palaces," appeared to take a page out of vaudeville's promotional playbook.

Perhaps most important, baseball and vaudeville both drew from the ranks of the uneducated and working class, and were generally more egalitarian than society at large, giving newly arrived immigrants and emancipated African Americans something they might not otherwise have had—a chance to display their talent. Nevertheless, there were still obstacles that even talent could not overcome.

Ethnic performers could change their names to fit in. Black performers, however, could not hide the color of their skin, although some did try. In a Jim Crow America awash in racism, few African Americans would ever realize their potential on the vaudeville stage. By the time the United States awakened to the injustice of segregation and took the long overdue step of integrating Major League Baseball, vaudeville was a memory.

From the beginning, vaudeville managers had understood that in the new culturally and ethnically diverse America, a successful enterprise would need to entertain a broad slice of society. There had to be something for everyone—variety—and the design of a vaudeville bill, with its comic and dramatic skits, its ethnic humor, and its animal and novelty acts, as well as the design of the theater itself, was a conscious effort to keep everyone—including children, white-collar women, and immigrants—entertained and comfortable.

In time baseball team owners would pull another page from the vaudeville playbook and enhance the experience of the ballpark, as Tony Pastor had the experience of going to the theater, by introducing entertainment and comforts to complement the game and attract a new audience.

Years after the footlights had dimmed at Hammerstein's, Keith and Proctor's, the Hippodrome, the Grand Opera House, and the Orpheum, the spotlights began to shine again in small, family-friendly ballparks across the country, in places like Charleston, Sioux Falls, St. Paul, and Omaha. Vaudeville, or at least something that looked a lot like vaudeville, was ready for a renaissance.

If there had always been a hint of vaudeville in baseball, it took showman Bill Veeck to unleash the potential of entertainment at the ballpark and to recognize that not everyone was there for the baseball game. His legendary promotions—exploding scoreboards, sirens, fireworks, weddings at home plate, and Disco Demolition Night—drew the crowds, thrilled the crowds, and paved the way for the pregame, postgame, and between-innings entertainment that today is a staple of Minor League Baseball and, to a lesser extent, Major League Baseball—entertainment that ranges from the eccentric (Superhero Weekend, Dukes of Hazzard Night, Prom Night, Christmas in July, and Thirsty Thursday) to the serious (Red Cross Night, D.A.R.E. Night, Armed Forces and Teacher Appreciation Days, and Night Out Against Violence) to the whimsical (autograph sessions with regular folks, "quiet" games where no talking is allowed, and Average Joe At-Bat, for which an appearance at the plate is auctioned off to benefit charity).

There are fuzzy team mascots, kids' clubs, and trivia contests. Minibats, rally towels, bobbleheads, autographed balls, and retro batting helmets are given away at the turn-style—an echo of Tony Pastor's door prizes, which included dress patterns, bags of flour, and even whole

A hint of its former opulence could still be seen as workmen demolished Keith's Theatre in Boston in 1952. The same fate was met by thousands of theaters nationwide as radio and television lured patrons away from the theater and urban renewal projects transformed city neighborhoods. (Photograph by Leslie Jones. Courtesy of the Boston Public Library, Print Department.)

pigs to entice women into the "new" vaudeville show. Ballparks across the country host youth clinics, clubhouse tours, Boy Scout campouts, Grant-Your-Baseball-Wish Nights, and Run-the-Bases Day (stroll the bases, for those over sixty!). And there are the national "acts"—such as BirdZerk!, Rubberboy, the Famous Chicken, Frisbee Dogs, Myron Noodleman, Zooperstars!, and the Oreos and Milk Tour—that travel the national baseball circuit, from small town to small town, just as their predecessors did on the vaudeville circuit a century ago.

Although *true* vaudeville's intimacy, sincerity, spontaneity, diversity, and sometimes utter absurdity—its unique artistry—did in fact succumb to radio and television, reports of vaudeville's death did not take into account the degree to which vaudeville, over its fifty years, had impressed itself on the American psyche and how its spirit would continue to influence entertainment for decades to come. In some ways, vaudeville never died.

The war years saw the vaudeville style reincarnated in United Service Organizations (USO) song and dance shows. Many of the pioneers of early radio and television were former vaudevillians who brought their old-time acts to the airwaves. By the 1960s and 1970s, vaudeville shtick— the sight gags, the cameo appearances, the "hook" (*The Gong Show*), the giggling dizzy dame (Goldie Hawn), the "nut" acts (Gladys with her handbag), the insult humor (Meathead and dingbat), the "rube" (Jed Clampett), the one-liners and catch phrases ("Sock it to me" and "You bet your sweet bippy")—had become a staple of sitcoms and television variety shows.

During the 1980s and 1990s Steve Martin could get a laugh every time he walked onstage with an arrow through his head. So too Chevy Chase with his pratfalls, Dana Carvey with his Church Lady impersonation, David Letterman with his stupid pet tricks, and Jerry Seinfeld with his show about nothing—all novelties right out of vaudeville's playbook. Even today a more recent incarnation of vaudeville can be seen on reality television shows such as *America's Got Talent*.

9

Exit Smiling

Norworth's song did more to popularize and sentimentalize baseball than any single factor in the game's history with the possible exception of Babe Ruth's fabulous bat.   JACK NORWORTH's obituary, quoting an unnamed baseball executive

In the years after "Take Me Out to the Ball Game" was written, Jack Norworth and Albert von Tilzer had the pleasure of knowing that their sunny, singable song with its simple, single syllables that captured so perfectly the experience of going to the ballpark had remained in the popular repertoire, surviving Americans' loss of innocence and the inevitable changes in public taste that occurred as the United States went to war, roared through the 1920s and Prohibition, endured the Great Depression, and went to war two more times in their lifetimes.

In part because Norworth was known to and admired by audiences as both a performer and a songwriter, he is more readily associated with "Take Me Out to the Ball Game" than is Von Tilzer (although Von Tilzer did occasionally grace the vaudeville stage to plug his songs).

Both men eventually saw their first professional baseball game—heard the crack of the bat and the roar of the crowd. Von Tilzer attended his first game sometime in the late 1920s and Norworth, as he later recalled, in the mid-1940s when, while living in Brooklyn, he attended a Dodgers game at Ebbets Field. If in the past he had been indifferent about baseball, that game at Ebbets Field, Norworth later said, had made him a fan.

After the success of "Take Me Out to the Ball Game" and his other

ALHAMBRA 7th Av., 126th.
Telephone
6000 Morn.
ALL CONCERTS TO-DAY AT 3:15
STAR & 8:15.
WEEK BE- TO-MORROW MATINEE
GINNING DAILY, 25c.
SPECIAL ENGAGEMENT. "HOME AGAIN."
NORA JACK
BAYES & NORWORTH
CADETS DE | CROSS & | PANTZER
GASCOYNE | JOSEPHINE | TRIO
Extra Feature | Extra Feature
THE LITTLE | BOWSER-
STRANGER | HINKLE & CO.
ARLINGTON FOUR | FERRELL BROS.
Added Attraction. JESSE L. LASKY'S
THE LOVE WALTZ

During their five-year marriage, Nora Bayes and Jack Norworth enchanted audiences in productions such as *Home Again*, advertised here in the *New York Times*.

hits during that magical year of 1908, Von Tilzer partnered with other well-known songwriters, including Junie McCree and Lew Brown, to write a string of hits, including "Put Your Arms Around Me Honey." By 1920 he had turned his attention to writing full scores for Broadway musical comedies, but as the stage musical and Tin Pan Alley declined, Von Tilzer moved to California (Tin Pan Alley West) to write for the talking movies. He retired in the mid-1930s and died in 1956 at the age of seventy-eight.

Jack Norworth too enjoyed success in the years after "Take Me Out to the Ball Game," particularly during the years he partnered with his wife, Nora Bayes, with whom he starred in and wrote for vaudeville and musical comedies (*The Jolly Bachelors, Little Miss Fix-It*) and recorded extensively for the Victor Talking Machine Company. After several years the Bayes/Norworth partnership began to fall apart, both personally and professionally, as Norworth was said to be growing increasingly impatient with what had become his onstage role as Bayes's "assistant and admirer."

In 1912, while living in Philadelphia, Norworth was stricken with acute Bright's disease, a kidney disease now known as nephritis, and was reported to be gravely ill, indeed near death. There being no treat-

AMERICA'S GREATEST COMEDY STAR

JACK NORWORTH

The celebrated Globe Galloper and his Company, with Harry De Costa at the piano, in an amusing, snappy, cleverly conceived novelty; such as only "Jack" himself is capable of presenting. A budget of new songs; and something doing every minute of his act.

After spending the war years in London, where he delighted audiences, Jack Norworth returned to New York where he was celebrated as one of America's very best entertainers. This 1920s ad welcomed the "Globe Galloper" home. (National Baseball Hall of Fame Library, Cooperstown, New York.)

ment for the disease at the time, Norworth traveled to Europe to take the cure in the healing baths of Carlsbad.

Late the following year, 1913, after his health was restored and he had divorced Bayes (and married Mary Johnson, an actress from the *Little Miss Fix-It* cast), Norworth relocated to London, where, billed as "the American boy," he performed throughout the war years. His immensely popular tongue-twisting ditties, "Sister Susie Is Sewing Soft Shirts for Soldiers," "Sister Susie Sells Sea Shells," and "Mothers Sitting Knitting Little Mittens for the Navy," delighted audiences and set the stage for the patter routines of the 1930s, one of the most famous of which was Abbott and Costello's classic baseball routine "Who's on First?"

Upon his return to New York in 1918, the "celebrated globe galloper" established himself as one of the best all-around entertainers, even becoming a New York theater owner, although the Jack Norworth Theatre was short-lived. "His name," noted one reviewer, "is one of the sterling-marks of the native theater." Another found him to be "as clever a story-teller off the stage as he is before the footlights." Still another called his act "perfect entertainment, as good as the very best of its kind."

During a two-decade career as a vaudeville headliner, he wrote hundreds of songs—by some accounts as many as 2,500—seven of which were good, in his opinion, including his two most famous, "Take Me Out to the Ball Game" and "Shine On, Harvest Moon."

"My songs do very nicely by me," Norworth once told an interviewer,

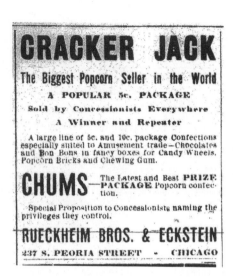

After relocating to California, Jack Norworth founded the Little League program in 1952 in his new hometown of Laguna Beach. In a 1955 letter, he wrote that he got "a big kick out of those kids." He soon began a tradition of handing out Cracker Jack, the popcorn, peanuts, and molasses confection that Norworth had immortalized in "Take Me Out to the Ball Game." Cracker Jack, featured here in ad advertisement in the *New York Clipper*, was first introduced by the F. W. Rueckheim Company at the 1893 World's Columbian Exposition in Chicago.

"because as soon as spring baseball training begins, the bands start playing 'Take Me Out to the Ball Game,' and that lasts right through the World Series. And then they start playing 'Harvest Moon' and that carries me through until spring again."

Jack Norworth was married two more times after his marriage to Mary Johnson. With his fourth wife, Dorothy Adelphi, Norworth performed for nearly twenty-five years and made a number of short films in the late 1920s and early 1930s. Ironically, the films were shown as fillers between vaudeville acts. A year after Adelphi's death in 1950, Norworth was remarried at the age of seventy-two to Amy Swor, the fifty-six-year-old widow of old-time vaudeville comedian Bert Swor.

Norworth retired gradually from the theater, collected royalties from

The distinguished and dapper Jack Norworth is shown here some years after he had written, at age twenty-nine, what would become baseball's anthem. (Billy Rose Theatre Division, The New York Public Library for the Performing Arts, Astor, Lenox and Tilden Foundations.)

Albert von Tilzer's partnership with Jack Norworth produced numerous Tin Pan Alley and vaudeville hits, although none more enduring than "Take Me Out to the Ball Game," published when Von Tilzer was thirty. (Billy Rose Theatre Division, The New York Public Library for the Performing Arts, Astor, Lenox and Tilden Foundations.)

Jack Norworth's signature. (Courtesy of Steve Adamson.)

his songs and, like Von Tilzer, moved to California, where he made occasional appearances in films and on radio and television, including visits to the Ed Sullivan Show and a final public appearance on Milton Berle's show. He became one of the country's foremost collectors of miniatures, his vast collection numbering more than twenty-five thousand pieces, including a catcher's mitt.

In 1952, in his new hometown of Laguna Beach, Norworth founded the Little League baseball program and became its honorary president. He began a tradition that year of personally distributing Cracker Jack to every young player on Opening Day, a tradition that his fifth wife Amy continued until her death in 1974 and that continues today. Laguna Beach Little League awards the Jack Norworth Trophy each season to the winner of the Majors Division.

In July of 1958, the fiftieth anniversary of "Take Me Out to the Ball Game," Norworth was honored with his own day at the Los Angeles Memorial Coliseum, home of the Dodgers, who relocated there from Brooklyn in 1958. In a pregame ceremony he was presented with a lifetime pass to any game played in either the American or the National League, an unprecedented honor.

"Handsome Jack" Norworth, known during his sensational career by many monikers—Happy Jack, The Heartbreaker, The Idol of American Youth, Jolly Jack, The Prime Minister of Mirth, and the King of Vaudeville—died in Laguna Beach on September 1, 1959. He was eighty years old. In 1970 he was elected, along with his "Take Me Out to the Ball Game" collaborator, Albert von Tilzer, to the Songwriters Hall of Fame.

Bibliographic Essay

1. THE EARLY YEARS

One can't, or shouldn't, attempt to write about baseball without first visiting the National Baseball Hall of Fame in Cooperstown, New York. Although resources in the A. Bartlett Giamatti Research Center were invaluable to the writing of this book, so too were the museum exhibits and the priceless artifacts that so vividly tell the story of baseball's early years.

The Library of Congress makes available online the full text of certain early *Spalding Official Baseball Guides*, and these, particularly the 1906 issue, provided a detailed background for the discussion about baseball's origins.

Ken Burns's epic masterpiece, *Baseball*, produced in cooperation with the National Baseball Hall of Fame for PBS in 1994, told the story of the game and, in that telling, the story of the United States. It is an invaluable resource for understanding how the past, more often than not, is prologue.

Finally, the words of so many *New York Times* reporters of yesteryear brought 1908 back to life. While reading about that year offers a profound sense of how far we've come in a century, it also reminds us that not all is changed. The human condition is the human condition.

2. THE NEW CENTURY

Several books provided a comprehensive picture of American life, innovation, and achievement during the first decades of the twentieth century. These include the *Our American Century* series published by Time-Life Books. The specific volumes consulted were *Prelude to the Century, 1870–1900, Dawn of the Century, 1900–1910*, and *End of Innocence, 1910–1920*. Another series consulted was the *American Decades* series—specifically *American Decades Primary Sources*—1900–1909 (Farmington Hills MI: Thomson, 2004), and *American Decades 1900–1909* (Detroit: Gale Research, 1996).

Equally enlightening was Alistair Cooke's *America* (Alfred A. Knopf, 1977) and the book's accompanying video series; and *America 1900*, produced by PBS (American Experience) in 1998. Key themes addressed in these resources include technology and invention, immigration, entertainment, race relations, and American colonialism.

3. LADIES AND GENTLEMEN, PLEASE TAKE YOUR SEATS

Many resources were consulted for a better understanding of the beginning, rise, and demise of early American amusement, Tin Pan Alley, and vaudeville. These include Leroy Ashby, *With Amusement for All* (Lexington: University Press of Kentucky, 2006); David Ewen, *The Life and Death of Tin Pan Alley* (New York: Funk and Wagnalls, 1964); Douglas Gilbert, *American Vaudeville: Its Life and Times* (New York: Dover, 1940); Joe Laurie Jr., *Vaudeville: From the Honky-tonks to the Palace* (New York: Henry Holt, 1953); Edward B. Marks, *They All Sang* (New York: Viking Press, 1935); David Nasaw, *Going Out: The Rise and Fall of Public Amusements* (New York: Basic Books, 1993); Charles and Louise Samuels, *Once Upon a Stage* (New York: Dodd, Mead, 1984); Anthony Slide, *New York City Vaudeville: Images of America* (Mount Pleasant SC: Arcadia Publishing, 2006); Anthony Slide, *The Vaudevillians* (Westport CT: Arlington House, 1981); Bill Smith, *The Vaudevillians* (New York: Macmillan, 1976); Robert Snyder, *Voice of the City* (Chicago: Ivan R. Dee, 1989); Bernard Sobel, *A Pictorial History of Vaudeville* (New York: Citadel Press, 1961); Karen Sotiropoulos, *Staging Race* (Cambridge: Harvard University Press, 2006); Charles Stein, *American Vaudeville as Seen by Its Contemporaries* (New York: Knopf, 1974); and D. Travis Stewart, *No Applause, Just Throw Money* (New York: Faber and Faber, 2005).

A number of video recordings helped to bring vaudeville and Tin Pan Alley back to life. These include *Vaudeville* (American Masters, 1997); *Show Business* (RKO Radio Pictures, 1944); *The Dolly Sisters* (Twentieth-Century Fox, 1945); *Yankee Doodle Dandy* (Warner Brothers, 1943); *Ziegfeld Follies* (MGM Musicals, 1946); *Coney Island,* by Ric Burns for the American Experience (PBS, 1991); and *Take Me Out to the Ball Game* (MGM Musicals, 1949).

Several websites were also very helpful to my research and my education on vaudeville. These include John Kenrick's cyber encyclopedia of musical theater, Musicals101.com. The site includes a variety/vaudeville category, profiles of theaters and performers, and research links. Parlorsongs.com, a site dedicated to the preservation of historical nineteenth- and twentieth-century musical manuscripts, includes an extensive composers section. Tinfoil.com, dedicated to the preservation of early sound recordings, including those on wax cylinders, includes an audio of Edward Meeker's 1908 recording of "Take Me Out to the Ball Game."

Several audio recordings were also very useful, including *After the Ball* (Nonesuch Records, 1974), a wonderful collection with a genuine vaudeville flavor, and cylinder recordings of vaudeville, minstrelsy, and popular songs, at Tinfoil.com.

4. 1908

In addition to Cooke's *America*, the Time-Life *Our American Century* series, and 1908 issues of the *New York Times* (microfilm), the audio CD titled *1908, Take Me Out with the Crowd* (Archeophone Records, 2004) provided a wealth of information in its liner notes and a selection of the top acoustical hits of the year.

5. BASEBALL AND MUSIC

The music files at the National Baseball Hall of Fame were most valuable in helping me to understand the role that music played and continues to play in baseball. Of particular interest at the Hall of Fame is an interactive exhibit where visitors may listen to numerous renditions of "Take Me Out to the Ball Game," including two of the earliest recordings, by Edward Meeker and Harvey Hindermyer.

An invaluable online resource for music, and specifically baseball music, is the superb Lester S. Levy Collection of sheet music at Johns Hopkins University. The collection covers the years 1780–1960, and the database is searchable by many categories, including subject, title, composer, lyricist, lithographer, and first line of song.

The Performing Arts Division of the Library of Congress also has an extensive collection of historic baseball sheet music.

6. TAKE ME OUT TO THE BALL GAME

John McCabe's 1973 book, *George M. Cohan: The Man Who Owned Broadway*, is an affectionate look at Cohan's forty-year, "star-spangled" career. Although there is a brief discussion of Cohan's love of baseball, no mention is made of his baseball song.

Indispensable to the piecing together of vaudeville performance routes were 1908 issues of the *New York Clipper*, the *New York Times*, *Variety*, and the *Brooklyn Daily Eagle*, all on microfilm.

Several resources helped to shed light on the personal and professional lives of Jack Norworth and Nora Bayes, as well as on the flavor of old-time vaudeville. These include the 1944 Warner Brothers production *Shine On, Harvest Moon*, starring

Ann Sheridan and Dennis Morgan. Although the movie is not an accurate portrayal of their marriage or professional careers, it captures the backstage intrigue and pace of vaudevillian life.

A much better sense of the two performers is found on *Nora Bayes and Jack Norworth, Together and Alone* (Archeophone Records, 2004), a double-CD compilation of fifty-one songs. Liner notes provide a detailed synopsis of the couple's partnership and their solo careers. Archeophone Records cautions that some of the material, although historically and socially important, may be offensive to modern sensibilities.

7. LET ME HEAR YOU GOOD AND LOUD

Correspondence with the late Skip Caray, son of legendary broadcaster Harry Caray, and Mike Veeck, son of Hall of Fame team owner Bill Veeck Jr. was most helpful in piecing together the story of Harry Caray and Bill Veeck's friendship and the "great gag" that immortalized "Take Me Out to the Ball Game."

Bill Veeck's memoir, *Veeck as in Wreck* (New York: Putnam, 1962), offers a fascinating backstage look at the fun and finances of baseball.

A commemorative audio CD, Harry *Caray, Voice of the Fans* (Pat Hughes, 2006), includes a classic rendition of "Take Me Out to the Ball Game" as well as a play-by-play of Caray's life and career.

The official websites for the Chicago Cubs and Chicago White Sox provide details of the two clubs' early histories.

8. BASEBALL AS VAUDEVILLE

The pages of *Variety* and the *New York Times*, particularly theatrical display ads in the latter, were helpful in piecing together the connections between baseball and vaudeville.

Numerous official team websites for Minor League Baseball were also helpful in understanding the vaudeville-like entertainment that is featured at ballparks across the country.

9. EXIT SMILING

Obituaries for Jack Norworth and Albert von Tilzer from various U.S. newspapers were helpful in piecing together the lives and careers of these two gentlemen, particularly their later years after they had left show business and the limelight.

The Locke Envelope Collection and photo files for Jack Norworth at the New York Public Library offered a wealth of material, particularly about the heyday of his career.

Correspondence by email with the Laguna Beach Little League organization helped fill in the details of Norworth's involvement with the league during the 1950s.